The CAROLINIAN MURDER at NAGS HEAD

The Janet Siclari Story

John Railey

Published by The History Press
An imprint of Arcadia Publishing
Charleston, SC
www.historypress.com

Copyright © 2025 by John Railey
All rights reserved

First published 2025

Manufactured in the United States

ISBN 9781467159173

Library of Congress Control Number: 2025931931

Notice: The information in this book is true and complete to the best of our knowledge. It is offered without guarantee on the part of the author or The History Press. The author and The History Press disclaim all liability in connection with the use of this book.

All rights reserved. No part of this book may be reproduced or transmitted in any form whatsoever without prior written permission from the publisher except in the case of brief quotations embodied in critical articles and reviews.

To use your talent as a writer to seek justice for those who are unable to defend themselves is one of the noblest quests there is. John Railey is one of those rare authors whose tireless pursuit of justice in three remarkable books (so far) is to be lauded. John has an amazing ability to reach into a complex criminal case to reveal the simple truth that was hidden there all along. Highly recommended!
—*Ira David Wood III, author, actor and former director of* The Lost Colony *outdoor drama on the Outer Banks*

*For Janet
And for Kathleen*

CONTENTS

Cast of Characters 9
Author's Note 11
Prologue 15

Part I: The Crime
  1. Lured by the Old Hotel 21
  2. Alone on the Beach 33
  3. The Crime Scene 42
  4. A Hell of a Hurricane 56
  5. Hunting the Murder Weapon 61
  6. A Master Investigator Takes on Suspect Randy Powers 65
  7. The DNA Breakthrough 80

Part II: The Reckoning
  8. Confronting Thomas Jabin Berry 85
  9. Jabin Berry Cracks 87

Part III: The Trial
  10. "The Horror of Random Chance" 101
  11. Matlock Enters the Courtroom 108
  12. Speaking for Janet 117
  13. The Defense Guns the State's Case 127
  14. Mother vs. Mother as the State Pushes for the Needle 133
  15. Life or Death? "The Rape of Innocence" 140

Contents

Epilogue 147
Acknowledgments 153
Bibliography 157
About the Author 159

CAST OF CHARACTERS

The Setting
The Carolinian hotel, Nags Head

The Victim
Janet Siclari

The Key Investigators
Detective Tom Gilliam, Nags Head Police Department
Agent Donnie Varnell, State Bureau of Investigation

The Key Suspects
Randy Powers
Thomas Jabin Berry

The Prosecutors
Assistant District Attorney Robert Trivette
Assistant District Attorney Amber Davis

The Defense Attorneys
John Graham
Mike Sanders

AUTHOR'S NOTE

In the early morning hours of Saturday, August 28, 1993, thirty-five-year-old Janet Siclari walked out to the beach in front of the venerable Carolinian hotel at Nags Head to smoke one last cigarette before calling it a night after partying with friends.

Janet's body was found on the beach in front of the hotel a few hours later, not long past daybreak. Her corpse, raped and throat slashed, was curled into a fetal position, facing north, toward her New Jersey home. The sea and winds were still calm, but Hurricane Emily was slowly moving in and hit the beach the following Tuesday night, destroying what was left of the crime scene and, with a mandatory evacuation order in place, giving witnesses and even, perhaps, the killer, license to flee. As a newspaperman, I drove down to Hatteras Island to cover the area Emily hit hardest, the town of Buxton, just over an hour south of Nags Head on the Outer Banks, our frail sand finger between the ocean and Sounds. I filed hurricane stories but never stopped thinking about Janet, a nice, beautiful Catholic girl who met an evil few of us locals had ever encountered.

An investigator with the Nags Head Police Department and another with the State Bureau of Investigation prevailed after a long journey to justice, thanks to their hard work and advances in DNA testing that were happening as the case unfurled. The lawmen's story is intriguing and powerful.

So is that of the defense attorneys for the man charged in the case. In trying to save their client's life, they pointed the finger at an early suspect in the case and battled talented prosecutors. It was straight out of *Matlock*, the

Author's Note

popular network TV series of the time that starred Andy Griffith, who lived right across the Roanoke Sound from Nags Head, as a defense attorney.

This book comes from interviews with numerous case insiders, lawyers, detectives, Dare County and state records and the trial transcript of the man ultimately charged with killing Janet.

All the names in this book are real except for Nora Martin, Carrie Purvis, Randy Powers, Faith Hopkins, Irshad Anderson, Susan Jones and Mary Smith. Those names are pseudonyms to protect privacy.

John Railey
Nags Head
May 2025

This is the end, this is the end of the innocence.
—Don Henley in his 1989 song "The End of the Innocence"

The Carolinian hotel is going to factor very importantly into this case.
—Defense attorney John Graham, in court in 1999

The wicked flee when no man pursueth; but the righteous are bold as a lion.
—Proverbs 28:1

PROLOGUE

Nags Head
August 28, 1993

The county where this crime occurred is appropriately named Dare. When Dare County was established in 1870, the Outer Bankers realized, like so many other Americans on the fringe before them and after, that they needed to establish a local government. It would be one that would set laws for them to live by, in addition to those of the far-off state and federal governments, and to get continued aid from those bodies, especially for their lighthouses and their heroic workers in the U.S. Lifesaving Service, the precursor of the Coast Guard. The local officials named their county after Virginia Dare. Today, road signs for those entering the county's Roanoke Island proclaim it "BIRTHPLACE OF AMERICA'S FIRST ENGLISH CHILD—1587," even though the signs give short shrift to the generations of American Indians born in the area before, including the leaders Manteo, Wanchese and Wingina. The Virginia Dare distinction became the calling card for the county, glorified in *The Lost Colony* outdoor drama, starting in 1937, that tells the story of the colony of Virginia Dare and her people vanishing in the late 1500s.

By the 1960s, as tourism blossomed, the county's name had taken on a new meaning for many: *Daring*, wild, seductive, a place to find yourself or lose yourself among legions of scantily clad, sun-seeking, sea-loving fun lovers on a sliver of sand in the summer, if only for a few days.

In August 1993, Janet Siclari met that culture.

On the last night of her life, she just wanted to say goodbye to the sea she loved, sitting on the beach, her favorite place to be in the whole world.

Prologue

Janet smoked a Marlboro Light, buried her suntanned toes in the sand and stared out at the Atlantic. The moon, coasting between clouds, was hitting full, on the eve of a rare Blue Moon. The temperature was a mild seventy-six, having dropped several degrees after the sun-kissed fun that Janet and her friends had shared frolicking on the beach the day before in front of the Carolinian.

Janet must have loved looking at that mysterious, majestic sea. In 1970, *National Geographic* magazine ran a story on the Outer Banks that included a map pinpointing more than five hundred ships that had perished just off the Banks in the Graveyard of the Atlantic, where the cool Labrador current meets the warm Gulf Stream over shallow banks, from the late 1500s through the late 1960s. The map became iconic, and copies were sold in Banks stores. Janet might well have seen the map.

Victim Janet Siclari. *Dare County Superior Court records.*

It's so comforting, so soothing to sit on the beach on a calm time like Janet's last one, that Saturday predawn, just listening to the waves softly lapping the sand, the sea oats standing tall, and thinking about the past and present, parallel time in a region where some locals, descendants of shipwreck survivors, still spoke in an Old English accent—*tide* was "toide" and *ice* was "ioce."

A mile and a half to the south of her seat was the iconic Nags Head pier. Near the pier, the USS *Huron* had floundered on the shoals on another Saturday, November 24, 1877. The naval ship had left the Hampton Roads area of Virginia the day before, headed to Havana to survey the surrounding coast. It hit a heavy southeaster and grounded on the shoals. Even though the *Huron* was only about two hundred yards offshore, the waves were breaking mean and cold, taking no prisoners. Ninety-eight souls perished, so close to shore.

Just to Janet's north, beside her hotel, was The Oceans condominium complex. Most, if not all, of its residents had left their balconies and gone to bed by then. Janet was alone, just loving her ocean, dreaming her dreams. There is a universality and camaraderie among those who love the sea. Janet's first love was the Jersey shore, but she, like so many others, loved the Outer Banks for its relative lack of heavy commercialization.

But the Outer Banks was rapidly changing in 1993, with developers buying up many of the old cottages and hotels, bulldozing those sweethearts and squatting garish McMansions in their place as old-line families, after quarreling among some, surrendered to the lure of big money and sold out. Some of the old oceanfront cottages around the Carolinian, her sisters, had yet to give in. Just a few cottages north of the Carolinian was one of the first A-frames on the northern Outer Banks, the "Gibson cottage," featuring a church-like stained-glass window. During parties in the 1960s, a surfing son of the Gibsons would sit at an organ by that gloriously lit window and play and sing a popular hit of the times, "Secret Agent Man," when his parents weren't around. On the north side of the Gibson cottage had been a beautiful, flat-topped turquoise cottage that patriarch Ezra Gibson built in the 1950s, following up on his A-frame beauty.

Janet knew the free-natured beauty of the beach but little of its violence, much less of the few killers who rarely roamed the sand.

A shadow descended over her. Janet was trusting, believing in basic good, maybe first trying to talk to the stranger. Then he attacked her. She stood just under five feet tall and weighed ninety-two pounds. But she fought back,

The Carolinian around the time of Janet's slaying. *Walter V. Gresham III.*

having once said she'd rather die than be raped. The killer prevailed. He ruined her, then took her voice, slitting her throat so bad he left her voiceless, cutting her jugular and her larynx cords, then slinking off and leaving her dying on the beach. Janet, an ultrasound technician, wasn't giving up. She grabbed the shorts the killer had torn off her and held them to her throat, trying to stop the bleeding, curling up and facing north, her lifeblood spilling out in the sand she loved. She might have tried to cry out for help, but the killer's cut had rendered her silent.

Others would rise to speak for her.

Part I
The Crime

Nags Head, North Carolina
August 28, 1993

1
LURED BY THE OLD HOTEL

This quiet dust was gentlemen and ladies
And lads and girls;
Was laughter and ability and sighing.
—Emily Dickinson, "This Quiet Dust"

The Carolinian's lobby was filled with beautiful rattan furniture, including couches where folks would sneak out from the basement bar to make out. They'd snuggle by the old pine walls like the generations before them, the ghosts dancing.

Janet Siclari loved the beach. She loved the sands of her native New Jersey and often ventured to other coasts, as well as ski resorts. She was a hard worker, becoming an ultrasound technician in North Arlington, New Jersey, after being honored for graduating at the top of her class in her training program. On vacations, she often ventured with her best friend, Nora Martin, to Atlantic City in Jersey and to California, Mexico and Vermont.

Nora, thirty-six, and Janet had bonded in high school over the fact that they were both the babies of their families, and both had three older brothers. They considered themselves sisters. When they were in their twenties, two movies set in their era, *The Big Chill* (1983) and *St. Elmo's Fire* (1985), defined the changes longtime friends went through after college as they sought to maintain their ties and pursued romance.

Wherever Janet went, those who met her were struck by her beauty. She was petite, with big eyes almost hazel, long brown hair, a ready smile and a welcoming nature. She was compassionate, loving and caring, always trying to help others.

In 1993, Nora and Janet planned a trip to the Outer Banks, drawing in Janet's brother Robert "Bob" Siclari and other friends, including Carrie Purvis. Bob and Janet were especially close. He was just two years older than her, and as the youngest children in the family, they had shared much, including sleigh rides in the Jersey winters. As Bob and Janet talked about

Janet and friends stayed in this rental cottage in Southern Shores the week before they moved to the Carolinian for one night. *John Railey*.

going to the Outer Banks, they agreed it was "a fun, safe place." Bob had been to the Outer Banks before.

The group secured two cottages for Friday, August 20, through Friday, August 27, in Southern Shores, a town near the northern tip of the Outer Banks. The women flew into the Norfolk, Virginia airport and secured a rental car for the drive of about an hour and a half south to the Banks.

Southern Shores, between the towns of Kitty Hawk to the south and Duck to the north, is beautifully landscaped and was planned generations before, with many distinctive flat-topped cottages and wide spaces between them, unlike the overdevelopment raging across most of the rest of the Outer Banks, especially the northern Banks.

Janet and her friends had a great week, playing on the nearby beach most days, cooking dinners at home, including barbecued chicken and Italian food, and venturing south. One night, they ate at Goombay's on the Beach Road in the town of Kill Devil Hills, a local eatery with a cozy bar.

Another night, they went for drinks at Kelly's in Nags Head, a restaurant and bar with rocking bands and dancing, a favorite of locals and tourists. Owner/operator Mike Kelly, a jolly, bearded beach legend who'd begun his career at two bedrocks of the Nags Head restaurant world, the Seafare and A Restaurant by George, weaved through the customers, welcoming them and charming them with tales of the Outer Banks, infusing them with knowledge that would make them feel like locals, if only for a week.

Early that week, Janet and some of her friends drove south to the island of Ocracoke, which Nora had visited in college and wanted Janet and the rest to see. They ate dinner there and caught one of the last ferries back north, a fun ride of approximately forty-five minutes across the Pamlico, one of the largest, most beautiful Sounds in the world. On the best days, dolphins cavort in the Sound by the ferry, salty sea spray delightfully hitting the passengers.

On the day the women drove to Ocracoke, Bob, a serious bicyclist, pedaled at least ten miles south from Southern Shores, going by the Carolinian, which he remembered had live music and other entertainment. When the women came back to Southern Shores from Ocracoke, Bob told them the hotel might be a fun place to hang out for a day on the beach, playing volleyball and flying kites.

On Wednesday afternoon, the group went to the Carolinian. Shimmering all flat-topped and bold between the big yellow dunes, the hotel, approaching fifty years old, was a gracious lady at odds with the new development near her. The Carolinian looked like something out of old Cuba. Janet and her friends quickly found that the hotel was fun, with volleyball games on the

Above: On one of the nights of the last week of her life, Janet ate with loved ones at this popular Kill Devil Hills restaurant, Goombay's. *Kathleen Railey.*

Opposite: On another night, Janet and her people dined and danced at the popular Kelly's restaurant in Nags Head. Owner/Operator Mike Kelly holds court in this photo. *Drew C. Wilson photo via the Outer Banks History Center, State Archives.*

beach and a fine sandbar. There was a waist-deep trough to wade or swim out through, then, a few hundred feet out, at low tide, knee-deep waters and, on the best days when the low tide agreed, waves to surf boards on or bodysurf into the beach.

Janet's "crew," as Nora called them, played volleyball and swam in the sea, delightful dips into the cool water after working up a sweat. They then shared drinks at the hotel's tiki bar, watching the waves and meeting the bartender, Randy Powers, a big, friendly and charming military vet with a sprinkle of tenacity and mystery: He had a prosthetic leg but revealed little of how he came to lose his real leg. He was tailor-made to the county of Dare and its daring nature of reinvention, having recently shucked off his Tidewater, Virginia roots.

Janet and her friends would have heard stories from Powers and others at the bar about Nags Head, the signature town of the Outer Banks, bordered by the ocean on the east and, just under a mile west across the slender finger of sand, the Roanoke Sound. The earliest settlers of the area, many of them shipwreck survivors, had settled in Nags Head Woods by the Sound, a wild and wondrous maritime forest with high bluffs over the water. They eked out a living through small herds of pigs and cows, hunting the surrounding deer and small game and casting nets from their boats on the Sound and the sea. They built their lives and they built their legends, including that of a witch who lived in the woods among them. They buried their dead in cemeteries that stand to this day.

In the days just before the Civil War, newcomers, wealthy farmers from northeastern North Carolina, some through enslaved Black labor, built resort cottages south of Nags Head Woods, on the Sound around Jockey's Ridge, a sand mountain. The newcomers rode in on steamships in those days before bridges. They partied by the Sound, their music riding the salt winds to the less fortunate back in Nags Head Woods. In those days, vacationers preferred the often-calm Sound over the often-rowdy ocean. But years later, these newcomers built cottages on the Nags Head oceanfront, an area that would come to be known as the "Unpainted Aristocracy" because the cedar-shingled cottages housing old-line families, often with wraparound porches, by design, lacked paint. The Carolinian was a few miles north of those cottages, which stand to this day.

The hotel opened in 1947. Beth Ownley Cooper writes in *The Historic Hotels and Motels of the Outer Banks* that "the Carolinian was one of the first hotels constructed on the Outer Banks during the post-World War II building boom":

It soon became known as Nags Head's most modern hotel. The structure included 64 rooms, all with baths and telephones, and a dining room that overlooked the ocean. Lucille Sermons [Winslow], her brother Wayland Sermons [from "Little Washington" North Carolina], and her sister and brother in-law Lima and Julian Oneto were among a group who developed the Carolinian. [Winslow] and the Onetos ran the hotel until 1969.

Ole Anderson, a nephew of Winslow who worked at the hotel in the 1960s, told the author,

Around the hotel, Lucille was known as the Silver Fox. When she showed up it was like a jolt of 220v-current hit the place—everybody stepped a little more lively and made sure their work was done properly once they heard she was on the premises. She truly was the heart behind the elegance and overall demeanor of the hotel while Julian and Lima did the day-to-

Poolside massages at the Carolinian in the 1960s. *Aycock Brown photo via the Outer Banks History Center, State Archives.*

Swimsuit competition at the Carolinian back in the day. *Aycock Brown photo via the Outer Banks History Center, State Archives.*

day to keep it running smoothly, which it always did. Even when the roof blew off the Dogwood dining room during Hurricane Hazel in 1954.

The hotel, which, by 1964, had become the largest on the Outer Banks, was closely tied to the Unpainted Aristocracy. The rich farmers who owned those cottages partied at the hotel. There, they joined friends from Manteo, the rest of the state, southeastern Virginia and, to a lesser extent, the rest of the nation as well. The hotel had become an Outer Banks bedrock, hosting art and fashion shows, fishing tournaments, kite-flying competitions and Jeep races on Jockey's Ridge. Julian Oneto, on guitar, led singalongs during beach bonfires on the Carolinian oceanfront, Cooper writes.

The Carolinian had small occupant rooms because it was designed to save space for big meeting rooms downstairs. It was the home of numerous events such as Valentine's Day foxhunts to spur on business in the offseason. Horses gave way to Jeeps and stock cars, racing through the sands of Colington Island and Nags Head Woods. The hotel hosted

The Janet Siclari Story

Above: The Carolinian dining room in the 1960s. *Aycock Brown photo via the Outer Banks History Center, State Archives.*

Opposite, top: Foxhunt launch at the Carolinian in vintage times. *Aycock Brown photo via the Outer Banks History Center, State Archives.*

Opposite, bottom: The Carolinian hotel during the Ash Wednesday storm of 1962. *Aycock Brown photo via the Outer Banks History Center, State Archives.*

annual meetings of the Man Will Never Fly Society, a lighthearted, hard-drinking locals' roast of Dare County's history as the birthplace of aviation with the Wright brothers' flight in 1903. The group's motto: "Birds fly. Men drink."

Legendary Outer Banks photographer Aycock Brown, who literally put the Outer Banks on the national map, luring in tourists, shot countless photos of Carolinian events and distributed them nationwide.

The hotel, "long considered to be the strongest building on the beach... served as the headquarters for media members who flocked to the Outer Banks when severe storms approached," Cooper writes. She notes that the hotel survived a horrific storm in March 1962.

That nor'easter, spurred on by a Spring Tide, was the worst storm the Outer Banks had endured since a hellacious hurricane in 1933. Ocean waters met the Sound waters in 1962, resulting in some heroic rescues, including those done by Nags Head store owner Carl Nunemaker in his airboat. The storm raged for three days. Aycock Brown, who tirelessly shot hundreds of photos of the storm damage, tagged it forever as the "Ash Wednesday Storm," a nod to his Episcopal faith, and most important, as a way of naming the storm, as opposed to named hurricanes, so officials would keep it high up in disbursing relief funds.

The Carolinian was the launching pad of the Pirate's Jamboree, a hard-partying gathering of men and women dressed in pirate garb, peeling out of the hotel parking lot in convertibles and parading south to Hatteras Island and then back to the Dare County seat of Manteo, where they climbed in boats for more parading and partying around Shallowbag Bay, the beautiful water that elbows around Manteo. The event ended in 1964 when it got too rowdy.

Luis Mesa, a gifted artist and immigrant from Cuba, held court for years in a corner of

Participants in the Pirate's Jamboree, a party launched from the Carolinian each year in the 1960s, in front of the Cape Hatteras Lighthouse. *Aycock Brown via the Outer Banks History Center, State Archives.*

the Carolinian lobby near the pay phone, painting portraits of the Carolinian owners and many others.

In the decades after, the hotel began a swan dive, the victim of new bars and new hotels with larger rooms.

But in the 1980s, the hotel, under the ownership of the Martin family from Virginia Beach, enjoyed a brief revival, a gray lady dancing, trying to be hip with events that included a popular bikini competition.

Top: The Carolinian in the late 1970s. *Walter V. Gresham III.*

Bottom: The Carolinian after a rare snow. *Walter V. Gresham III.*

Bikini competition at the Carolinian in the 1980s. *Drew C. Wilson photo via the Outer Banks History Center, State Archives.*

Her basement bar, with popular R&B bands, reggae bands (and patrons slipping out on the beach to smoke pot) and comedy acts, drew crowds. In the early 1990s, the basement bar, under manager Anita Fletcher, became a full-time comedy club, hosting many popular acts.

Constants remained. The Carolinian's lobby had an old-time switchboard, with multiple wires clerks used to plug into phone service in the rooms like something out of film noir. The lobby was filled with beautiful rattan furniture, including couches where folks would sneak out from the basement bar to make out. They'd snuggle by the old pine walls like the generations before them, the ghosts dancing.

And outside, on the oceanfront, was one of the gray lady's newest and best attractions, her tiki bar, a spot Janet and her friends quickly grew to love. It was atop the high sand dune the old hotel enjoyed. After a day of play on the beach, it was a prime spot to kick back, drink, watch the ever-changing Mama Sea and meet new friends.

2
ALONE ON THE BEACH

I'm going back out. I'm going for a walk.
—*What Janet Siclari may have said to her brother in the early morning hours of August 28, 1993*

As Janet and her friends checked out of their Southern Shores cottage on the morning of Friday, August 27, they talked about how their flights back to Jersey out of Norfolk weren't until the next day around noon. In those pre-9/11 days, there were no extensive check-ins for flights. Patrons could show up moments before boarding time without fear of losing their seats.

Janet and her friends chatted and decided to stay in an Outer Banks hotel for another night because the weather was so nice, with the hurricane still days away. They checked out one potential lodging but found it not to their suiting. Then someone said, wait a minute, we loved the Carolinian crowd, let's stay there. They drove a bit farther south in their rental cars, easily booking two adjacent rooms for Friday night on the third floor, including an oceanfront room on the northeast corner of the hotel, the best the Carolinian offered. Nora and Carrie would be in one room. Janet and her brother would be in the oceanfront room.

The group had a fine time that Friday, playing volleyball on the beach all afternoon, then easing the heat with jumps in the sea, calm that day. Sailboats and surfers played, and farther out, charter boats cruised past. Jets occasionally roared overhead from nearby military bases, as well as

Coast Guard helicopters, and small planes flew banners advertising restaurants and other businesses. That was cool to watch, but best of all was the natural scenery, dolphins diving and rising, pelicans cruising by like little B-52s, gliding down to smooth landings on the water and diving in to grab fish with heavenly splashes before soaring off with wiggling prey tight in their beaks.

Janet, her group and the new friends they met added to the scenery, good-looking young women and men playing together, scantily clad and sneaking peeks at each other.

They drank at the Carolinian tiki bar as the sun set to the west, reuniting with the bartender, Randy Powers. In between serving drinks, he was playing backgammon with his girlfriend, bar manager Faith Hopkins.

Janet shortly before her murder. Dare County Superior Court records.

Powers told Janet and her group that he was going to the Port O' Call restaurant and bar that night, that it was a cool place to go, and the music was usually good there.

Janet and her girlfriends showered, blow-dried their hair and sprayed it to get it just right. They then had a leisurely meal in the busy hotel restaurant. They talked about hating to leave the beach. For a while, they went to the crowded bar in the basement of the hotel to hear a comedy act, then decided to follow Powers's tip on the Port O' Call, about two miles north, in the adjacent town of Kill Devil Hills. Janet's brother decided to stay at the hotel.

As Janet, Nora and Carrie walked to the Carolinian parking lot, two guys, one a hotel employee, followed them out, flirting with them before they left for the Port O' Call in Nora's rental car. The men shook their hands, and one kissed Janet on the cheek. One of the men told the women he had seen them on the beach earlier in the week and had been trying to talk to them.

The women laughed the men off and drove toward the Port O' Call, stopping to withdraw cash from an ATM, which the northern women called a "Macmachine." Janet did not withdraw any money. She had twenty-five dollars, she said, and that would see her through.

In their rental car, Janet and her friends drove the short distance north on the Beach Road to the Port O' Call. The two-lane road was dark. The road is sometimes shrouded by misty fog when the warm air from nearby Jockey's Ridge meets the cool air drifting off the Atlantic, but on this night, there were some clouds but not the mist. Traffic on the road was light, a few lonesome drunks stumbling by the road, a couple of stray dogs and cats wandering, their eyes catching red in the headlights, frogs chirping from the nearby weed-smothered ditches. Through their rolled-down windows, the women could have caught the smell of pot burning, joints passed among friends outside their cottages, and the cool sound of dogs howling at the full moon.

Aerial shot of Kill Devil Hills around the time Janet was murdered. *Walter V. Gresham III*.

It was the weekend before Labor Day, traditionally a time of sparse business on the Outer Banks, with longtime summer visitors holding off to visit until the Labor Day weekend, when they would kiss the summer farewell. Up until the 1990s, the weekend before Labor Day had long been a special time for locals, when they could set aside the summer rush before the last hurrah, a time to renew old acquaintances and maybe meet some new friends before the last-minute frenzy of Labor Day and the months of fall and winter when they'd have to make their seasonal earnings last until spring.

The Port O' Call, a sprawling two-story brick building on the west side of the Beach Road, dating back decades, was trying to hang on, just like its sister to the south, the Carolinian.

The Port O' Call opened in 1965, and was once known for being one of the more upscale seafood restaurants on the Outer Banks, not quite up to Owens' or the Seafare in Nags Head, but decent in its own way. In 1976, the original owners of the restaurant sold Port O' Call to Frank Gajar, who later added a gift shop and a second-story saloon to the venue.

The Port O' Call in its heyday in the 1960s. Thirty years later, it was one of Janet's last stops. *Aycock Brown photo via the Outer Banks History Center, State Archives.*

The Port O' Call around the time of Janet's murder. *Archival photo.*

The restaurant hosted many charity events, Amy Pollard Gaw notes in her book *Lost Restaurants of the Outer Banks and Their Recipes*. Under Gajar, the bar booked some good bands, including the Connells, a great power-pop act out of the North Carolina state capital of Raleigh.

A velvet-red color saturated the bar area. The bar, remembered sometime-patron Bennett Rose Payne, was like a cross between Liberace and Dolly Parton.

At the Port O' Call, Janet and her friends climbed carpeted stairs to the second floor, where they settled down into plush chairs and watched a younger crowd dancing below.

The top hits of that year would have been playing through the sound system, including Rod Stewart's cover of "Have I Told You Lately That I Love You?," UB40's version of "Can't Help Falling in Love with You" and the dreamy remix of "What a Wonderful World" and "Somewhere Over the Rainbow" by Israel Kamakawiwo'ole. There also might have been some Mariah Carey, Bon Jovi, Boyz II Men and Aerosmith.

Above: On the last night of her life, Janet and two girlfriends climbed this stairway to the second floor of the Port O' Call bar. *Author photo of the interior of the Port O' Call in September 2024.*

Opposite: Janet and her friends took seats here on the second floor of the bar. *Author photo of the interior of the Port O' Call in September 2024.*

Nora drank water because she was tired. Janet had a rum and coke, then a Rolling Rock beer in its distinctive green long-neck bottle. Janet might have lit up one of her Marlboro Lights in those days when you could still smoke in bars. A man came up to them, kidding that they should come downstairs and "socialize."

From their seats, Janet and her friends watched dancing below until they descended and joined in. *Author photo of the interior of the Port O' Call in September 2024.*

The man left. Janet and her friends agreed they were being "blobs" and would go downstairs. But Janet said, "Oh, I hate these guys that wear baggy pants and these skinny little guys."

The women went downstairs. They saw the bartender from the Carolinian, Randy Powers, and his girlfriend, Faith Hopkins.

Nora and Carrie soon told Janet they were tired and wanted to go back to the hotel. She and Carrie would walk back there, Nora told Janet, and gave her the keys to her rental car. It was a pretty night with a nice moon, a good night for a walk, Nora said. Janet wasn't drunk, Nora would later remember.

A CAROLINIAN WORKER SAW Janet walk into the hotel about 2:45 or 3:00 a.m.

Shortly thereafter, Janet went into the hotel room she shared with her brother. He heard her key in the lock and awakened. "It's only me," Janet said. Bob was glad to hear his sister was home and thought she would climb into her twin bed and go to sleep. But she told him, "I am lighting a cigarette." She may have also said, "I'm going back out, I'm going for a walk," Bob would later say. She pulled a Marlboro Light from her pack on the dresser, struck a match and lit it. You could still smoke in hotel rooms then.

As his sister opened the door to leave, Bob could hear voices in the hallway, but the hotel room TV was on, so the voices were indistinct. He thought his sister was just stepping outside to smoke and everything was fine. He went back to sleep.

3
THE CRIME SCENE

The lawmen were facing a hard case, a real who-done-it, aggravated by all the foot traffic on the scene the day and night before. The challenge was further aggravated by the fact that a hurricane named Emily was moving toward the Outer Banks, set to arrive Tuesday night.

Vincent Lamont Freeman had worked for the town of Nags Head's public works department for about five years. Early on the morning of August 28, the town's crew emptying garbage cans at public accesses to the beach was shorthanded. Freeman volunteered to help out—hard, thankless work.

It was a hot, muggy morning, typical for Nags Head in the dog days of August. Shortly before 7:00 a.m., as they approached from the public access just south of the Carolinian, Freeman saw something at the bottom of the steps leading down from the hotel. He shouted out to a coworker. "There's a woman up there that is half-naked laying on the beach!"

Freeman got out of his truck and walked toward the woman to see if she needed help. As he approached her, he saw what looked like blood around her. He told his coworker, "Well, let me go call the paramedics because she might have had too much to drink or something like that."

But before calling, Freeman walked closer. The body was in blood-soaked sand, ten to fifteen feet away from a set of wooden steps leading up to the hotel. Freeman saw the woman's eyes were still open. He bent down and looked at her and told his coworker, "This woman is dead, man. Her eyes aren't blinking.'"

Top: Public beach access, today, just to the south of Janet's crime scene. *Kathleen Railey*.

Bottom: The site of Janet's crime scene today. The Oceans condominium complex is to the immediate right. *Kathleen Railey*.

Freeman called a supervisor: "It looked like somebody gave her a tissue or something to try and stop the bleeding.…The way she is laying it looks like she's been in a fight or something. She's laying in a puddle of blood. I didn't touch anything."

Freeman's supervisor called Nags Head police. At 6:49 a.m., a dispatcher sent out a radio call: "Report of possible dead or injured woman near Carolinian."

Patrol officers soon arrived and cordoned off the crime scene; shortly thereafter, the on-call detectives, Tom Gilliam and Ben Whitehurst, arrived.

They saw the body of a small woman curled into a fetal position, lying on her left side, facing north. Clad only in a blue denim vest, she clutched a pair of blood-soaked off-white shorts to her throat. A belt lay beneath the body. There was a lot of blood around the neck and face and upper portion of the body and on her legs.

There was a laceration on the left side of the face. There were deep cuts to the throat. There was a wristwatch with a leather band on one wrist, a silver bracelet on the other wrist. There was an empty paper bag near the body.

There was no purse, keys or wallet around the body. Beside the body were liquid pockmarks in the sand, as if someone had urinated or poured something out. It had not rained. Footprints were everywhere, as the point where the body was found was heavily traveled.

Whitehurst sketched the crime scene. Gilliam snapped photos of it. There was a pair of high-top tennis shoes about twenty-five feet from the body, near the bottom of the steps to the Carolinian. The beige Spaulding shoes, size 9 medium, men's, had a pair of gray socks stuffed in them. The shoes would become crucial in the case. To find the killer, the detectives would have to find the wearer of those shoes. It was, as others would call it, a Cinderella case.

Gilliam, in his early thirties, became the primary investigator on the case for his department. He was from nearby Virginia Beach, Virginia, and had majored in criminal justice at Western Carolina University in the North Carolina mountains. He had always loved the Outer Banks and had begun working for the Nags Head Police Department right after college. He had made detective just six months before Janet's case. He is of medium build and height, earnest, soft-spoken and hardworking, prone to listening rather than talking, staring folks straight in the eye, traits that would serve him well on the case.

Nags Head Police Detective Tom Gilliam during an interview with CNN's *Forensic Files* TV series.

As Gilliam surveyed the crime scene, he called his friend Robert Trivette, an assistant district attorney who lived nearby, and told him he should come to the beach. Trivette was there within minutes.

AROUND 8:00 A.M., BOB Siclari awakened and saw his sister was not in her twin bed and that her unzipped suitcase still sat on top of her bedspread, which had not been turned down. He was concerned. But maybe she had crashed in the room next door with her girlfriends because they had stayed up late chatting, he figured.

Then he looked out his window, saw the yellow-taped crime scene on the oceanfront and officers and got a sick feeling in his stomach. He raced over to Nora and Carrie's room and banged as hard he could on their door. From what he had seen on the beach, he had a gut feeling that something had happened to his sister.

The women answered the door.

"Where is Janet?!" Bob asked.

They told him, "Well, she is not here, we thought she was with you." Bob ran into their room, looking around. When he didn't see his sister, he knew something had happened to her. Nora and Carrie went to Bob's room, noting that her sandals and pocketbook were still there. "Bob, look, she was just here. Maybe she went for an early morning walk on the beach," Nora said.

On the dresser were two packs of Janet's Marlboro Light cigarettes, one not all the way empty, the other with one cigarette missing from it.

In a panic, Bob left his room and ran down the stairs toward the beach. Three police officers held him back. Bob told them, "I need to get to the beach. Something happened. My sister is missing." Finally, an officer told him, "It's a young girl, a young girl is dead."

Bob kept screaming that he needed to get to the crime scene. The officers wouldn't tell him anything.

Nora and Carrie ran down the steps to the beach, asking questions. Officers continued to hold Bob back. Panic and confusion set in for Bob and the women.

The officers asked Bob how tall his sister was, how much she weighed and if he had a photo of her. He gave the height and weight to them, but did not have a photo of her with him. The grueling process seemed like four hours to him, Bob would later say, but it was probably only about forty-five minutes or an hour.

An officer started questioning Nora and Carrie. Nora found the questioning, over and over, left her numb: What happened? What did she look like? What was she wearing? Did she wear jewelry?

Nora kept asking if the body was that of a woman.

"We don't know it's your friend at this point," one of the lawmen told her.

Meanwhile, Lieutenant Cliff Midgett, a cool professional over Gilliam and Whitehurst, arrived and supervised. The officers on the beach continued to work the crime scene, surrounding it with personnel to prevent rubberneckers peeking in, but that was difficult. From an oceanfront balcony at the Oceans condominium complex, next door to the hotel to the north, onlookers were gazing down.

Trivette, the assistant district attorney whom Detective Gilliam had called, surveyed the crime scene. Trivette would later say that the investigators working the scene knew how to do their jobs better than he did. The Nags Head Police Department, headed by Chief Lonnie Dickens, was a good one.

Trivette later said he went to the Carolinian "because every good prosecutor wants to see the crime scene. It's motivation. I wanted the image burned in my head to fuel my fire to find Janet's killer. I never forgot that image."

The investigators finished their preliminary work on the scene, doing their best to gather as much evidence as soon as possible. They took a look at Nora's rental car in the south end of the Carolinian parking lot, the one Janet had apparently driven home from the Port O' Call. There was a Miller Lite

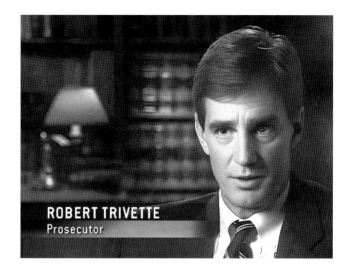

Dare County Assistant DA Robert Trivette responded to the crime scene. *CNN's* Forensic Files *TV series*.

beer can beside the driver's door and one by the passenger's door. There was a brown cigarette butt inside the car, on the passenger side. The investigators sent the beer cans and cigarette butt to the SBI lab for testing.

The lawmen were facing a hard case, a real whodunit, aggravated by all the foot traffic on the scene the day and night before.

The challenge was further aggravated by the fact that a hurricane named Emily was barreling down on the Outer Banks, set to arrive Tuesday night. A mandatory evacuation was looming. And here they were on Saturday morning, with the clock ticking too fast. There was no sign of the storm yet, but it was definitely coming. The crime scene, what there was of it, would soon be washed over. The killer, as well as potential witnesses, might well flee the beach under the evacuation order. And as the hurricane set in with all hands on deck dealing with it and offices closed, the lawmen's investigation of the case would be severely limited. Landline phones might well crash, a severe handicap in those days before widespread cellphone use.

Janet's body was placed in a black bag for transport to Twiford Funeral Home in Manteo for the local coroner's exam. The officers soon had Bob Siclari in a car with them for the trip to the funeral home.

Nora and Carrie watched. Through his rolled-down window, Bob yelled to the women, "Come with me please!"

He had overheard officers saying that the victim was about five feet tall. He knew that something had happened to his sister.

Officers soon told Nora, "All right, come with us, we're going to take you to the body." Nora got in the front of a police car. Carrie got in the back.

The officers started driving the women to the funeral home. Along the way, it hit Nora: *We are going to identify a body. We told the officer what Janet looks like. So the body must be hers.*

At the funeral home, with lawmen milling around, Bob Siclari, thinking Janet was still alive, asked, "Where is my sister? What room is she in?"

A priest pulled him aside and said, "You know, we don't know this, but if it is your sister, you know, can we say a prayer? Are you religious?"

"Yes, I am," Bob said. He and Janet were raised as Catholics. He and the priest knelt down and said a prayer. Bob knew that something tragic had happened.

Then, Nags Head Police Officer Jimmy Ray Watts led Bob to a room where his sister's body, dressed only in a blue denim vest, was on a stainless-steel gurney. Two steps into the room, Bob knew it was his sister. Her hair was matted with blood, and blood covered her face. He tried to move closer to the body. Two lawmen held him back and pulled him out of the room.

His face told all to Nora and Carrie, who were devastated. "It can't be. It just can't be," Nora said.

Bob talked to the lawmen, deciding he needed to call his relatives. He got through to his parents in New Jersey with the terrible news.

One detective told Nora and Carrie: "You have to start to remember everything and everybody that you talked to this week, everything."

Nora told the lawmen, "We need to catch a flight."

A detective said, "I think you are going to be here a while. We are going to impound your car, so we need you girls here, probably for another night."

The officers drove Bob and the women to the Nags Head Police Department on the Beach Road, about six miles south of the Carolinian. Detective Chris Catron asked Bob about everything he and his sister had talked about, everything they did, when the last time he saw her was, if he saw her with anybody who looked suspicious or who looked intently at her. There were some suspicious-looking people at the hotel, Bob said, waiters and people who worked there. He was suspicious of everyone, he said, including Randy Powers, the Carolinian bartender.

Bob told the investigators about Janet entering their hotel room early that morning. "She lit a cigarette. I remember that because I smelled it. And I think she was talking to somebody because it sounded like she was talking to someone like, 'Wait a minute.' You know, I heard this, like whispering, and I am like half asleep and she said something like 'It's just me' or something, you know, and I remember her lighting a cigarette. She left her cigarettes because I saw them before I left. It looked like a new pack of Marlboros, Marlboro Lights. But it definitely sounded like she was with somebody because she wouldn't, you know, have just come in and left."

As other investigators began talking to Nora and Carrie, Nora went blank. Carrie yelled at her: "Start thinking and start helping!"

Nora settled down, and she and Carrie spent several hours detailing their week for the lawmen, including first going to the Carolinian on Wednesday. The only people they really met, they said, were Randy Powers, the Carolinian bartender; his girlfriend; and a couple from the hotel tiki bar Friday night who, along with Powers and his girlfriend, showed up at the Port O' Call.

The lawmen asked the women about Janet's love life. Nora told them Janet had, successively, four boyfriends. The first one was when she was about twenty, Nora said, and ended after about a year. Then she had lived with another man for about eight years. After that relationship ended, she dated another man for a short period. For the past three years, Nora said, Janet had been with "the love of her life," but she couldn't get a commitment from him and feared he was unfaithful to her. Lately, their relationship had been "on and off."

Janet had a fear of being raped, Nora said. Once, she said, as she and Janet rode to a Vermont ski trip with another friend, that friend told them about a woman they knew who was raped. Janet got upset, Nora said, and said she would never allow anybody to rape her; she would rather die first.

Finally, at 10:00 p.m. that Saturday, the detectives told the women they were done going over their rental car and they were free to go.

Nora and Carrie called their parents to tell them the bad news and to let them know that they would be a day late. Letting them know they'd be late seemed especially important now.

The lawmen drove the women back to the Carolinian. The women climbed the stairs to their room and quickly packed. There was no way they were spending the night there. They got in the rental car and drove north toward Norfolk, a far different journey than their happy one just days ago, coming to the beach with Janet. Somehow, they worked their way to a hotel near the Norfolk airport and flew out the next day.

Meanwhile, other Nags Head officers canvassed the Carolinian, interviewing all the guests and gathering phone numbers for guests who had departed.

Earlier that same Saturday, the detectives, at their Nags Head department, had begun their first of several interviews with Randy Powers, the Carolinian bartender, starting by knocking on his front door with Faith

Hopkins, the Carolinian manager and Powers's girlfriend. Powers came to the door.

A body had been found on the beach behind the Carolinian, they told him. They didn't know if it was a drowning or what, they told him. Then Faith told him: "It was the person you were with last night, Randy."

Randy Powers, the Carolinian bartender who was a suspect in the case, lived in this block in Nags Head, pictured in August 2024, just a few hundred yards from the Carolinian. The small cottage he rented was demolished to make room for larger cottages. *Author photo*.

Powers responded, "Janet?"

Faith answered, "Yes."

Powers said, "I have got to get up there [to the Carolinian] because she dropped me off last night."

At the hotel, Powers told the investigators about riding home with Janet. The investigators took a brief statement from him. Powers told the investigators that he had been drinking that night.

A second interview happened later that day, at 5:10 p.m. at the Carolinian. Detective Chris Catron conducted that interview with Detective Ben Whitehurst. Whitehurst began, telling Powers that "what I want you to do now is start from the [Carolinian] deck yesterday."

Powers rolled through the day's events, describing seeing Janet and her friends at the Carolinian tiki bar he tended the previous night and then seeing them at the Port O' Call. He talked about getting a ride back from Janet to his house, near the Carolinian, and that all was well when she let him out. Catron told Powers: "Like I said, this is nothing unusual, and I don't want you to get uncomfortable.…In something like this, we got to go through all the hoops. I mean we really got to push." The interview continued:

Powers	You talk about uncomfortable. I mean, I feel extremely uncomfortable, but it's really a moot point. It's something I got to do.…It's just hard for me to fathom this whole thing. I mean I'm really having a hard time even trying to make this thing real. It doesn't make any sense.
Catron	I don't know what they should do with somebody who does something like this.
Powers	No, I definitely…in my opinion, shoot somebody that does something like this.
Catron	Well, maybe they will bring back hanging one day.
Powers	Maybe, maybe they will find a way that's better, but I don't know. I just hope that somebody is found because.…You know, I'm scared s——less after this whole thing. I'm the last one that saw her.

Catron	Well…
Powers	I don't know how anybody else would feel, but I just, I just right now, I mean I feel like dog shit.
Catron	Well, that's understandable.
Powers	All I can hash through is saying "be careful" is the last thing I said to her.
Catron	Well, that's all you can do is, not warn them, but at least…
Powers	I would have never, never would have expected this in Nags Head. That's all I did with them [Janet and her friends] the whole time they were down. I just kept saying the same thing [that it was a safe place.]
Whitehurst	Yeah, but other than just the every-once-in-a-while conversations that you had there [with Janet] there was no other relationship between you all?
Powers	None whatsoever. None whatsoever.

The interview ended.

Shortly thereafter, detectives interviewed Faith Hopkins. She told them she was not Powers's girlfriend; they were seeing others, and Powers was too possessive of her. She was dismissive of Powers, sometimes to the point of nearly laughing him off.

―――

THE LOCAL CORONER RULED Janet's death a homicide. Her body was transported to a state medical examiner's office in Greenville, North Carolina, that Saturday, a drive west of less than two hours from Nags Head.

Dr. Page Hudson did the autopsy, starting just before 3:00 p.m. on Saturday with Detective Gilliam present. Hudson was well respected. Best-selling true-crime writer Jerry Bledsoe of North Carolina wrote this about

Hudson in his 1991 book *Blood Games*, about a 1988 murder in nearby Washington, North Carolina, called "Little Washington" by locals:

> Dr. Hudson had been North Carolina's first chief medical examiner, a job he'd held for eighteen years. He had stepped down to teach, write, research and garden, but he still liked to take up the scalpel, the bone saw, and other tools of his trade now and then in intriguing cases. Although he had been an effective administrator, creating the state's system of medical examiners and establishing databases to help law enforcement agencies investigate homicides, suicides, and different types of accidents, he relished the role of medical sleuth above all others. He had conducted more than four thousand autopsies, many of murder victims, and he was a noted authority on arsenic poisonings. He even had discovered a new technique for detecting arsenic in the body. Despite all that he had seen, he never ceased to marvel at the horrible things that humans can do to themselves and to one another.

Bledsoe's competitor on a book about that 1988 murder, Joe McGinnis, provided further description of Hudson:

> Page Hudson was fifty-nine, and a native of Richmond, Virginia. He'd been educated at Johns Hopkins and Harvard….Dr. Hudson was a large man both physically and in reputation. He stood six three, had thick white hair, and spoke in a deep, commanding voice, which, while never overbearing, exuded both knowledge and authority.

Hudson would file his written report on Janet's autopsy a month later, but he gave Gilliam details as he worked. According to Hudson's written report, Janet was just under five feet tall and weighed ninety-two pounds. He noted:

> Much blood on body particularly head, neck and chest. The only clothing is a vest-like object. There is a deep suntan excepting a small bathing suit area. No scars are noted. No bite marks are found. No evidence of injury is seen about the genital area. A moderately long hair is stuck by blood to the palm of the right hand. The fingernails are short and no material is seen trapped beneath the nails.

By "WOUND DESCRIPTIONS" on the autopsy form, Hudson wrote:

There are five (5) sharply incised wounds about the neck, two of these are on the upper left neck, beneath the corner of the jaw.... The direction appears down and forward.

He noted the deadly wound: "This is a deep and penetrating wound and is contiguous with the traverse cut across the larynx and the cut into the left jugular vein.... There was marked blood loss."

Hudson would later testify that there were a few cuts about her neck, most notably two-and-half-inch cuts that went deep, through the larynx, just under the vocal cords. One of her two jugular veins, the one of the left side, was almost severed. It was about half cut through. Hudson thought that was the wound, with the resulting loss of blood, that killed Janet.

The larynx wound caused a considerable amount of blood to flow into Janet's lungs, Hudson would later testify, and the blood in the lungs told him Janet may have lived for several minutes after the stabbing. She had swallowed blood, as Hudson found it in her stomach. The superficial wounds to her neck may have been "compliance" or "intimidation" wounds, Hudson testified. Those wounds may have been caused by the killer holding the knife to Janet's throat to subdue her.

Hudson noted in his autopsy:

There are several incised wounds on the inner aspects of the fingers.... The wounds on the inside of the hands represent so-called defense wounds [she'd tried to fight off her killer]. *No injuries are seen about the genital area, but spermatozoa were frequent as seen on vaginal smears.*

Hudson did not find evidence of trauma in the vaginal area but said it's not uncommon in sexual assaults not to find trauma.

Hudson determined that Janet's blood alcohol level was .08, the starting threshold for driving while impaired in North Carolina. Janet was no drunkard, as normal standards on her liver showed. At ninety-two pounds, a few beers would have easily taken her to the .08 level. A great irony in her case: If she had just been pulled over for driving while impaired, a constant threat for partiers in Dare County, especially those driving late at night, she would probably still be alive today.

By "PATHOLOGICAL DIAGNOSES," Hudson wrote:

> *Multiple cut and stab wounds of the neck*
> *Cut of left jugular vein*
> *Transection of larynx*
> *Pulmonary aspiration of blood*
> *CAUSE OF DEATH: Loss of blood from cut and stab wounds of the neck.*

Catron and Gilliam were assigned the case.

4
A HELL OF A HURRICANE

Mama Sea and her accompanying winds rock and roll, caring nothing for the duties of man. Thus it was for the lawmen working Janet's case. The Carolinian survived, as she always had.

The news of Janet's murder rocked the beach, even as Hurricane Emily barreled in. She had developed just six days before from a tropical wave northeast of the Lesser Antilles, an island group in the Caribbean almost two thousand miles from the Outer Banks. She was the fifth named storm of the 1993 hurricane season. The season runs from June through November.

Locals did their usual storm preparation, including boarding up windows, securing boats and pets and parking vehicles on high ground. As they worked, news of Janet's murder spread quickly through word of mouth, the beach grapevine, including through Carolinian workers, even though the local newspaper, the *Coastland Times*, would not report it until its next edition on Tuesday.

Locals instinctively understood Janet's attraction to their sand. It was the beach-loving freedom they had long enjoyed, and they realized that freedom was contagious to people like Janet from the North, where beach access is often restricted. Beach freedom is sacred on the Outer Banks. Feeling safe on the sand at night, from violence and even broken glass, was taken as a given. At the numerous free beach accesses along the Banks, locals routinely slip off their flip-flops and sandals at the base of the access steps to walk barefoot in the sand and that footwear is never stolen.

But older locals realized Janet had joined a long line of mysteries and violence, from the clashes between the Indians and lost colonists in the 1500s to shipwrecks off their coast like the one in the early 1800s in which Theodosia Burr Alston, the daughter of Aaron Burr, allegedly perished.

In July 1967 on Roanoke Island on the Outer Banks, the "Summer of Love" in other parts of the country, Brenda Joyce Holland was strangled and, quite possibly, raped. Her body was dumped in the Croatan Sound. Her slaying remains unsolved, despite strong evidence that pointed to her killer.

Twenty-seven years later, in February 1990 on Roanoke Island, Stacey Stanton, who lived on the same street as Brenda in Manteo, just several houses over, was found fatally stabbed in her apartment. A man was wrongfully convicted in her murder. Just like Janet, Stacey was from Jersey. Their crime scenes were separated by the Roanoke Sound between Roanoke Island and Nags Head. But they were sister victims.

There are ghosts who dance beside us on the beach, mysteries, visitors and locals doomed together in ways they'd never realize on this side of eternity.

Janet reminded us of this. The violence and the mysteries, the ghosts dancing between here and now, the quick and the dead.

THE TUESDAY AFTER JANET'S body was found, the investigators had to take a break as Hurricane Emily headed in, expected to make landfall that night. Mama Sea unfurled increasingly larger waves, crashing onto the beach and mankind's fragile strivings, including Janet's carefully yellow-taped crime scene. The Nags Head lawmen had to help other town departments prepare as well as secure their own homes. As they did so, they worried about suspects and witnesses fleeing the hurricane.

The front page of the *Coastland Times* broke the story of Janet's slaying that Tuesday morning, but quietly, due to the pending storm. The story about Janet's death ran on the front page with a headline of "Body of Tourist Found on Nags Head Beach," but it was only five paragraphs long, buried beneath stories about Hurricane Emily.

Emily's timing was terrible for tourist season and for the investigation. The hurricane was threatening to shut down, or seriously inhibit, business the next weekend, that of Labor Day, the last big moneymaking weekend of the summer. One of the newspaper stories featured above the one about Janet's slaying reported that officials had ordered a mandatory evacuation of Dare County. Such orders are rarely prosecuted. Dare County law enforcement officers have never dragged people out of cottages and into cars for transportation off the beach. But the evacuation orders do carry an ominous warning: Officers sometime caution those who won't evacuate that they won't be coming out in the midst of the storm to save them, that they will be on their own. How many body bags should we plan on for you all? the officers sometimes ask.

For many tourists and some locals, such words are enough to send them scrambling for the long evacuation lines. But many locals stick it out, concerned with a variety of issues, ranging from not wanting to leave their pets behind to not wanting to face the traffic jams returning to their property. They're used to hurricanes, they've lived through many and they can survive the next one, even though a full-scale hurricane hadn't hit the Outer Banks in years. Locals develop a bravado.

That Tuesday morning at ten o'clock, Janet's family held a funeral mass for her at Sacred Heart, their Catholic church in Lyndhurst, New Jersey. Janet's obituary noted that she was survived by her parents, Damy Daber and Anthony Siclari, as well as her brothers and "numerous nieces and nephews."

The church was packed, with people even sitting outside. There was much loud crying. "I just wish I could get her back," her mother would later say.

She and Janet were close. Recently, they had been to Paris together. They visited the French Riviera and shared much laughter and long chats "about everything. There was no secret between Janet and me." Daber later recalled:

> *She said, "Mom, I will never get married. I wish I would find somebody nice." And I said, "Janet, it's not meant for everybody to be married, not meant for everybody to have a child. You could always adopt," talk like that to make her feel better, but she wanted to be married, to have a family like her two brothers. She really wanted to.... What hurt me the most, I bought a little condo in Florida and she loved the sun so much and she'd say, "Oh Mom, when you go there I will have a suntan all year round." She said, "I will be with you in the wintertime, I will be there."...She never had a chance, but I have that room, I call it Janet's room.*

Later that Tuesday, Emily hit peak winds of 115 miles per hour as she headed to the Carolina coast.

Top: The Outer Banks in the aftermath of Hurricane Emily. *Drew C. Wilson.*

Bottom: In a Nags Head storm shelter, a boy watched news of Hurricane Emily as the storm roared south toward Hatteras Island. *Drew C. Wilson.*

While glancing off the Northern Outer Banks, part of her eye passed over southern Hatteras Island, a forty-five-minute-drive south from the Carolinian. She came in with high tides and the full moon. There was massive flooding from the Pamlico Sound in the Hatteras village of Buxton.

Then Emily slowly weakened, eventually heading off Bermuda and dying a few days later off the wild coast of Newfoundland.

Emily spared Nags Head for the most part, but her rising tide and heavy beach erosion erased what was left of Janet's crime scene.

5
HUNTING THE MURDER WEAPON

On September 8, with the hurricane gone, Detectives Tom Gilliam and Chris Catron reinterviewed Randy Powers at the Nags Head cottage where he lived. The cottage was about a quarter mile north of the Carolinian, on the west side of the Beach Road. Powers told them he had served more than four years in the army and lost a leg in an accident in 1985. He had a prosthetic leg. He had been working at the Carolinian since the previous April, he said.

The night Janet was killed, Powers told the investigators, two friends were staying with him, a policeman from New York and a respiratory therapist from the nearby Tidewater region of Virginia. That night, he said, he went home after work and showered before going to the Port O' Call.

At that bar, around midnight, he told the investigators, he saw Janet and her friends with a couple they had met at the Carolinian. He got mad, Powers said, because a man was dancing with his girlfriend. Meanwhile, he said, he noticed that Janet was dancing with someone who seemed "a little goofy, it didn't seem like somebody Janet would be dancing with."

Powers's girlfriend Faith walked to the parking lot. Powers followed her out and had words with her. She "took off with somebody," Powers said, and he walked back in the bar.

His cop friend told Powers he was tired. He wanted to get home and would come back for Powers if needed. Powers told him no, that he would take a cab.

Then, Powers said, Janet said she would give him a ride home. He told her he'd take a cab. Distracted by the argument with his girlfriend, he told the investigators, he wasn't in a talkative mood. Janet repeated her offer of the ride. Powers finally took her up on that. He said he did so because a man Janet had danced with said he'd let her drive him home, and Janet obviously didn't seem too thrilled about that. "It was like Janet was signaling 'ride home with me so I can get rid of this guy' and the guy got the message," Powers told the investigators.

As he and Janet were leaving, Powers said, "Janet gave the guy a hug or a peck on the cheek. She was just really nice to him, and it was done. I think she made her point without being rude and it was very classy and nice the way she did that, but he still got the message."

This was right around last call, Powers said, around quarter to two. They got in Janet's car for the five-minute ride down the Beach Road to Powers's cottage. "She seemed to be in tune to the fact that I wasn't very happy with my current relationship with Faith and was more or less consoling me," Powers said. "I mean it was just 'Oh, you guys will be OK, just don't let it bother you' that kind of stuff but I was really kind of just wanting to get back to the house."

The investigators asked him if he had smoked in the rental car Janet was driving. He said he had not, that he'd never smoked.

When Janet pulled up at the cottage where he lived, Powers said, he told her good night and thanked her for the ride. He watched her car pull away, headed south, toward the Carolinian a short distance away.

After she let him off at his house, he said, he went inside, then started thinking he wanted to go back to the Carolinian, where Faith lived on the first floor of the hotel.

Powers said, "I asked one of my guests if I could borrow his car because I wanted to head up to the Carolinian to see when and if Faith got in. My car had died, I believe the day before."

It's unclear why he didn't just walk the quarter mile to the Carolinian. As it was, he was risking a drunk-driving charge.

Powers said he hopped in the car, taking a stick of pepperoni and a steak knife to cut it with, and drove to the Carolinian. "I parked, backed into a parking spot which I guess would be at the north end of the parking lot. Just backed in so I could see when Faith came in."

In response to questioning by Detective Catron, Powers said he backed the car he was using by a boat on a trailer so that Faith wouldn't see the car.

Powers said he waited in his car for about twenty-five to thirty minutes, and he was extremely angry. He said he saw a woman pull up, park her car and get out, fumbling with her purse. At first, he said, he thought it was Faith but then realized it was Janet as she walked into the lights in front of the hotel. Powers watched Janet, by herself, walk into the hotel.

In later questioning, Powers said he was sure the woman who walked into the hotel was Janet, not Faith, because Faith was about five feet, four inches tall, four inches taller than Janet, and had "a little bit more meat on her" than Janet.

Powers told the investigators he got out of his car and walked to Faith's door, checking the door and making sure she was not answering. He was planning to break in through her window, as she had previously allowed him to do, and surprise her when she got back, he said.

A few minutes later, he said, he drove his friend's car back to his cottage and walked back to the hotel "because I still wanted to see what was going on with Faith." Then, he said, Faith drove up. He walked up to her car, he said, and they argued over what had happened that night:

> *I was standing in her car door, she was sitting in the car. She was telling me to get out of her face, more or less. And she pushed me in the gut and I kind of tapped her on the face, side of the face. And that pretty much sent her into a screaming rage.*

Faith stormed into the hotel, Powers told the investigators, and he walked home. His cop friend was "glad to see he was back and in one piece," Powers said, and he went to sleep about 3:30 a.m.

The investigators gathered three blue-handled steak knives from Powers's cottage for SBI testing.

The next day, Gilliam drove more than four hours to deliver the knives to the SBI lab outside Raleigh. The SBI found no blood, or indications of blood, on the knives.

Assistant District Attorney Robert Trivette, who had responded to the crime scene and was working closely with the detectives, read over the latest interview with Powers. He'd later say, "It was so bizarre, you couldn't make it up," with Powers freely telling the investigators about sitting outside the hotel, slicing up his pepperoni as he waited for his girlfriend to get home.

Starting on September 9, 1993, Detective Gilliam interviewed several Carolinian employees. Some of them lived in the hotel, on the bottom floor, which employees nicknamed the "Dungeon" and the "Pond," short for the

Ponderosa ranch of the popular TV Western of the 1960s, *Bonanza*. The employees included those who had flirted with Janet and her friends before they left the hotel for the Port O' Call hours before Janet was killed. Henry G. "Shawn" Herpin, who was the night desk clerk at the hotel, came on at 10:00 or 11:00 p.m. and stayed until the early morning. Herpin had been a popular local radio DJ known as "Shawn at Dawn" but had fallen on hard drinking. He often slept on the job, a fellow employee said, leaving the front desk unmanned, including on the night Janet was killed. During a long interview, Gilliam pressed Herpin, who claimed New Orleans law enforcement experience, and Herpin replied:

> *I'm capable of killing somebody, there is no doubt in my mind about that. That particular person ah…who perpetrated this crime I would have no compunction at all.…I don't think I could attack a woman.…I don't think I could do that. I don't know. I don't think I could.*

The investigators secured a blood sample from Herpin and cleared him.

On September 14, 1993, about three weeks after Janet's body was found, a Carolinian employee called the investigators to say a knife wrapped in a towel had been found in the bottom of a laundry bin that had not been emptied since before the murder. Laundry was done in a separate building to the hotel's south side. It's uncertain why that laundry had not been emptied for three weeks.

The find was especially intriguing, because the Carolinian employee in charge of the laundry room was one of the men flirting with Janet before she and her friends left for the Port O' Call on the last night of her life. And that employee had done time in prison on a voluntary manslaughter conviction.

Detective Gilliam responded, gathering the knife and checking out the laundry bin, finding the knife wrapped in a towel with dark stains. The knife had a black plastic handle and a nine-inch blade with a serrated edge. Gilliam sent the knife to Dr. Page Hudson, the pathologist who had done Janet's autopsy, asking him to examine it to determine if it might be the murder weapon. Meanwhile, Gilliam researched similar knives, finding they are called "tomato knives," good for slicing tomatoes and other food.

Dr. Hudson came back with a reply: The knife could have been the murder weapon, but he couldn't say for sure.

Interviews with the employee in charge of the laundry room, including luminol tests on his quarters at the Carolinian and blood tests on his body, proved fruitless. The investigators cleared that employee.

6
A MASTER INVESTIGATOR TAKES ON SUSPECT RANDY POWERS

So that's basically it, a person can either conceal or they can falsify, but if they do one or other they're going to indicate that. And that's exactly why I'm here, is to deal with that.
—*Master interviewer Don Rabon beginning a late September 1993 interview with Randy Powers*

At the Nags Head Police Department in late September, Don Rabon, who was not associated with the SBI but did technical assistance for the agency through the North Carolina Justice Academy of the North Carolina Department of Justice, took a run at Carolinian bartender Randy Powers at the request of the local investigators. At forty-seven, Rabon was at the top of his game, the ultimate "good guy" in interviews that often drew out all. He'd been educated at North Carolina's Davidson County Community College and East Tennessee State University, had military experience with the U.S. Army and had advised law enforcement agencies on interrogation and investigation across the United States and the world.

Don Rabon, who assisted the SBI in interviews on the case. *Don Rabon.*

Rabon taught law enforcement officers classes on interviewing suspects. Nags Head Police Detective Tom Gilliam had taken one of the classes and respected Rabon. Rabon began by emphasizing to Powers that he was "free to go at any point." Under that condition, that Powers clearly understood he was not in custody and free to go at any point, Rabon was not required to read Powers his Miranda rights, entitling him to a lawyer.

Rabon would have made sure that Powers had easy access to a door and could take a break whenever he wanted and leave whenever he wanted. As the interview began, Powers was moderately friendly, although, Rabon would later remember, Powers "wasn't going to kiss me on the cheek or something." Even though the interview was noncustodial, Rabon said, it was still intrusive to Powers.

As Rabon began, he told Powers that his "specialty is interviewing people, determining if a person is 100 percent honest":

Rabon	If a person is less than 100 percent honest, they've got two ways to go. The first way they can go is they can conceal. Meaning that there could be things that happened that they take out and they don't tell.… Or the other way that a person can be less than 100 percent honest is that they can falsify. Meaning that they can lie. That they can put something in there that doesn't belong there, or they can move things around. So that's basically it, a person can either conceal or they can falsify, but if they do one or the other, they're going to indicate that. And that's exactly why I'm here is to deal with that. So I want you to know, I'd rather you be a hundred percent honest with me, or if we move into an area you don't want to talk about, raise your hand.
Powers	Yes sir.
Rabon	I've read over your interview with Detective Catron here, and [have] a couple of things that I want to talk to you with in reference to that.…
Powers	Okay.

Rabon then went to great lengths to make sure that Powers was OK with talking to him, that he had slept well the night before, that he wasn't hungry or thirsty, and that he didn't need to use the restroom, commenting,

"You know, and being honest, you should be the most comfortable person in the room."

Rabon	So, if you will, before we get started, if you'll just tell me something about yourself. I would appreciate it.
Powers	I'm, ah, thirty years old, retired Army. I lost my leg in an auto accident in 1984. I've been bartending pretty much ever since.…Right now, I'm kind of at a point where I'm traveling around, not wanting to commit to any one job right now…and kind of enjoying it. Um, other than that, I don't know what I can tell you. I, um, think I'm pretty much a, ah, normal 30-year-old who's not married and no children.

After those "pleasantries," Rabon asked Powers to walk him through his activities around the time of Janet's death. Powers told Rabon that, as he arrived for work at the Carolinian about 11:30 a.m. on the Friday before Janet's body was found the next day, he saw Janet and her crowd checking in to the hotel, "And it was a pleasant surprise for me, because they had been on my [tiki bar] deck for the past few days."

When he got off work, Powers said, he caught a ride to the Port O' Call with a friend, not driving himself because he'd been drinking. He saw Janet and her friends there, he said, and saw his girlfriend, Faith Hopkins, dancing with another man and had words with her. He told Rabon about Janet giving him a ride home and then going to the Carolinian and waiting for Hopkins to get home. He was planning to sneak into her quarters through her window and then having words with her when she arrived home. He told Rabon about his anger at Hopkins and their tangled relationship: "My relationship with Faith is very simple. It's rough, it has been from the beginning. Um, basically, ah, Faith, you know, I find her very intriguing. Very nice. Probably one of the most enjoyable people, especially girlfriends, that I've ever had to be around."

Then Powers got into the complications. Faith has an ex-boyfriend who was in an accident and has some brain damage, Powers told Rabon, and "he is not quite all there" and "it seems to me that [Hopkins] has always felt that, ah, she has to take care of him in some way." Once, Powers said, the ex, while drunk, had confronted Hopkins and "threw her around," scaring her and hurting her "pretty bad."

A few minutes later, Rabon lasered in on Powers's problems with Hopkins and the violence associated with those problems. Powers admitted to confronting the man Hopkins was dancing with at the Port O' Call and grabbing his arm, then later confronting Hopkins in the Carolinian parking lot and slapping her.

Rabon	Apparently, you know, the frustrations have continued to build on your part…
Powers	Yes they have.
Rabon	Because the relationship is not what you would like for it be, and there is this continual ebb and flow of attraction rejection.
Powell	Right.
Rabon	So I can appreciate your, your frustration in that regard.
Powers	I mean, it's just, it's just too much. Um, you mentioned my ah, um, slapping her and getting angry, that's something I don't ever want to be a part of and don't ever want to do and it's, it's gotten to the point where it, ah, it's just, I'm the kind of person that a situation seems that bad I get out of it. I should have done this a long time ago.

Rabon told Powers he understood. "Tell me about, Janet," he said. Powers did so, coming across as a world-weary, cynical pusher of drinks.

Powers	Okay, well, as far, all I can tell you about Janet is that, you know, really it, I, as a bartender, I pay attention to a lot of things.
Rabon	Uh huh.
Powers	But names and specifics, um, I don't, I just pick up things here and there because I have to talk to a lot of people a lot all day long to make money.

> And that's basically what it's all about. I mean, you might not want to talk to somebody at all, but you have to, to make them happy enough to tip you.

He talked to Janet a bit, he said, when he was waiting on her and her friends at the tiki bar at the Carolinian.

Powers   And you know, the extent of our conversation that I recall was her asking me about me about my leg and then going into the fact that she had a motorcycle and her brother didn't like it. And that was probably the big thing that I really can recall from my conversation with Janet. Um, you know, to be perfectly honest, the next day....I didn't even know her name....And the conversations in Port O' Call were almost nil. I mean, you know, other than "how you all doing" and I, you know, have a tendency to go "how you doing hon" and, you know, "sweetie" rather than worry about knowing their names. That's exactly how I get around it.

Rabon   Sure. Uh huh.

Powers   So, I, I would say the extent of the conversation with Janet or any, any dealings with Janet was probably at most at that one point on the deck where she spoke about her motorcycle....And, you know, she loves it, riding down the road when people see, "God, that's a girl on a motorcycle." And the way she felt about that....That was about the extent of it. Um, Janet, Janet as a person, I, I found her and her other friend, ah, you know, slightly attractive. Not, not overly attractive. Uh, they seemed like very nice young ladies. Uh, full of a lot of energy. Fun kind of people it seemed like. Uh, but other than that, that's about my only impressions of her, with her.

Rabon	The information from, from her girlfriends, was that she was interested in, in you. Did she ever make a point…
Powers	Well, maybe, maybe, maybe that's exactly why she was making comments about Faith near the end, and when we were driving home. About you guys make a good couple. You shouldn't be upset. Umm, you know, I don't recall exactly what she said, because, like I said, I wasn't really paying attention. I was not in the mood to pay attention.
Rabon	So you were mad.
Powers	Right. And, and it was basically, basically as far as I can recall it was just comments, you know, "you guys make a good couple, don't let yourself get all upset," you know, and she, in a way, she kind of thought it was cute, but…even then I didn't sense that, that she had any interest in me. I just sensed that it was, you know, a typical person that you just met a few days before that's, you know, trying to be friendly and, you know, helpful. Trying to help you cool down a little bit.
Rabon	Uh huh.
Powers	Nothing more than that. I never once sensed that she had any interest in me. Um, at all.
Rabon	She never…did she make any sexual overture towards you?
Powers	Oh no, no, no. None whatsoever. Never, never, never leaned over looking for a kiss, or anything. Not that I would have been paying attention to…
Rabon	Uh huh.

Powers	…Never was there a, uh, move made by either of us…
Rabon	So you …
Powers	…toward each other.
Rabon	You were so focused on Faith and your anger was in regard to her
Powers	Yeah. Right
Rabon	For jerking you around, that…
Powers	Right, I wasn't paying attention to anything that was going on, or, you know …
Rabon	Uh huh.
Powers	…I wasn't totally furious. I was just preoccupied. And you know, you, I think that, uh, you got to understand exactly how things went. You take your, your kind of seeing me as though I'm very furious, and when Faith shows up I walk up and slap her. That's not the case. The case is, is that when I came up to the car and started to question Faith, she started doing her typical, you know, "you don't own me," you know, "you don't tell me what to do" and this and that…not once offering any information on who the gentleman was she drove home with. And when she went to pull away from me, I grabbed her hand and she ripped it away, and that's where I just went like that and tapped her right there.
Rabon	Uh huh. Was it on the right-hand side or the left-hand side?
Powers	Uh, it would be on her right-hand side.

Rabon	OK.
Powers	Because it was where she had, she had just had some, um, surgery so I felt even more bad after that, because I knew that I had hit her where she had just had some surgery.
Rabon	Dental surgery?
Powers	She just had a root canal.
Rabon	OK.
Powers	…I mean there is no justification…but it was not the kind of thing that was meant to, to hurt her at all. It was just to get her attention more than anything, because it was just like that.
Rabon	Uh huh.
Powers	But because of where it was, it hurt her and she was extremely pissed. But what I'm getting at was that I was more preoccupied in trying to find out what Faith was up to. The thing with me, and I've explained that to her before, is I want to see that something is going on.
Rabon	Uh huh.
Powers	I want to confirm that something is going on, so that I can say "fine." I'm not going to beat up anybody. I'm not going to jump into her because it's, I'm not going to end up getting thrown in jail for her or anybody.
Rabon	Uh huh.
Powers	But what I want to do is confirm it.

Rabon	Uh huh.
Powers	I may say some sweet things, but I'm, I'm not going to get involved in anything.
Rabon	Uh huh.
Powers	And that's all I wanted to do is to confirm that…
Rabon	[A few minutes later] So that's why you were angry. You were wanting to take the screen off [Faith's] window.
Powers	Right, right. I was going to stay in there and wait for her to come in.
Rabon	What would have happened if she would've come in there with another guy?
Powers	Then I would have known. I would have walked right out.
Rabon	What would you have done?
Powers	I would have walked right out. I, I mean Faith's right. I don't own Faith.
Rabon	Uh huh.

Powers told Rabon that he had seen Faith's car "over there where her boyfriend stays" and "I don't go running up there, and you know, the thing about the window, Faith has told me numerous times to go in her window to get this or to get that." In response to a question from Rabon, Powers acknowledged he had to use a screwdriver to get in the window. Powers circled back to his contention that he just wanted to "confirm" if Faith was "running around" because "it's the embarrassment of all these people who have seen us all summer together" and "always being together."

Rabon	Have you ever gotten so mad that you either said or did anything to her one night and not remembered having said it the next day?
Powers	I, I have no idea. I mean, we've gotten in some sweet little arguments where I'm sure there was something I've forgot I said, but I don't ever remember doing anything to her other than that slap. And you know, as far as I'm concerned, it's not something I'm, I'm really proud of.
Rabon	I understand.

Rabon turned to Janet giving Powers a ride home from the Port O' Call. He asked Powers about the two Miller Lite beer cans found by the rental car, the cans, Rabon said, that were "being processed now.…Would there be any reason that your prints would be on them?"

Powers said there was no reason his prints would be on one of the cans, that he didn't have "anything to drink once I left the Port O' Call" and "I don't drink Miller Lite anyhow."

A few minutes later, Rabon asked Powers to "speculate with me a little bit.…Why would somebody do this to Janet? What do you think? I wondered, maybe you have too. Why would somebody do something like this?"

Powers	I, I have no idea. I mean, I don't, I don't know why anybody would do that to anybody, but I don't, I don't know Janet. I don't know anything about her… but it's obviously a very sick individual and I don't know. I've never asked and don't particularly want to know what the, what the specifics of this thing are. Of course, everybody's got their scuttlebutt running around about what happened.
Rabon	What's the scuttlebutt?
Powers	Well I've heard, I've heard that she was raped. I've heard that she was bludgeoned. I've heard she was stabbed. I've heard she had her throat slit. I mean, there are so many people talking, you know.…

A few minutes later, Powers speculated about a man Janet had danced with at the Port O' Call who was "hounding her that night. I mean, she is a very nice person, by the way, you know, turned him down [to give him a ride home] and gave him a peck on the cheek....When I first came in [to the bar] I thought they might have known each other, because the whole group was standing together. But later, as the evening went on, and the way she came up to our group, I could tell that, that wasn't the case."

Rabon	We'll look at everybody that's involved in that perimeter.
Powers	Right.
Rabon	Who could have done it? Looking at everybody… who could have done it?
Powers	I, I have no idea. I mean out of everybody that's involved, the only people, the only person that I could think that could have done it would have been the guy that was hounding her, and uh, even though I don't want to uh, um, put anybody on the burner.

Powers also mentioned two men who worked at the Carolinian. A few minutes later, Rabon asked Powers, "What do you think ought to happen to a person that did this?"

Powers	Well, I think, uh, I, I think they should definitely be, uh, put to death....And that's exactly, exactly the way I feel now and when you ask me what should be done to the person, I'm thinking, oh great, I'm condemning myself, if I ever get wrongly convicted or if anybody else I know does.…
Rabon	Well, this is just speculation.
Powers	Alright…I know, but, but, you, you, I, I hope that isn't a, a, a uncommon fear. I would think that anybody that is, is as close to it as I am by seeing her last, by having words with my girlfriend in the

parking lot of the place, you know, would feel the same way.

Shortly thereafter, Rabon told Powers not to "worry about any of these questions because these questions are no different from…what we ask to anybody on this peripheral." Then Rabon dropped his bombshell, asking Powers if he was "involved" in Janet's death. Powers said he was not.

Rabon	OK. What would you say if I told you that I didn't believe you.
Powers	I, I'd say I'd do anything to prove to you to believe me. I mean, I don't know what to, what to say to you or what to do to make you believe me, but I would do anything that uh, that I could do, to prove to you that I'm telling the truth.
Rabon	Well, I'm not saying that I don't believe you.

Powers said that it would upset him "if I felt that, that somebody leading this investigation doesn't believe that I had nothing to do with the murder." In response to a question from Rabon, Powers said he would cooperate with the investigation. He added that he felt guilty for encouraging Janet and her friends to stay at the Carolinian. "You know, I told them how safe it was here. How much I love this area, because I'm from Newport News, Hampton [Virginia] where you can't even be nice to people."

Rabon let Powers talk a bit more along those lines and then sprang back.

Rabon	Do you think that it's possible that you lost your temper so badly that night that you could do something like this and not remember it the next day?
Powers	No siree. No siree. I, I, I got to tell you that the only, the only time that uh, that I even come up with a situation where I would forget things that I said would be if I had something to drink.
Rabon	Uh huh.

Powers	But even then, if, if I'm pissed off, I become fairly clear, and fairly lucid. I mean, for example, from the time I, I didn't even get there till midnight at Port O' Call, but I had a few good drinks, and I tipped the bartender, so they gave me good drinks....But from the time that the ordeal with Faith came on, I can tell you that I was as sober as I've ever been.

Powers rattled on. Rabon listened. The interview ended soon thereafter.

Rabon had lived up to his reputation as a master interviewer, putting Powers at ease, all but befriending him as he elicited information about his anger that night, keeping Powers comfortable so that he didn't stop the interview and invoke his right to a lawyer.

As Rabon walked out of the interview room, he met the local investigators, who asked him what he thought. Rabon told the author in July 2024 that he had provided an opportunity for Powers to make a confession. Powers had not done so. Rabon told the investigators in 1993: "Boys, I just don't think he [Powers] did it."

Rabon remembered in 2024:

> *The investigators didn't jump up and down, but they were willing to listen to what I had to say. I knew* [Powers] *was a person of interest and my feeling was that they were really looking at him, never closeminded. Eliminating the innocent is just as important as getting the guilty....My feeling was that he* [Powers] *didn't do it based on the totality of the interview, and he admitted to me he left some things out. You can't fall in love with a theory. A theory is all well and good and you got to have that, but if you're not careful, confirmation bias* [tunnel vision] *can kick in....You've got to be open to the idea that anything you think is wrong.*

Soon after the 1993 interview, Powers told a friend he was terrified that he would be implicated in a murder that he did not commit. He should have ended the interview before it started.

The investigators gathered blood from Powers for DNA comparison with the semen found in Janet's body, as well as blood from several other Carolinian employees who had spoken with Janet. They got no hits, including from Powers, whom they effectively cleared from any involvement in Janet's slaying.

Trivette would later describe Powers as "an overgrown kid…trying to hang onto his 20s, but not a killer."

Still, Powers had taken a big chance by talking so freely to the investigators without a lawyer, who would have told him to shut his mouth. What he'd said in the interviews would later come back to haunt him as other parties became involved in the case.

As fall closed in, the Carolinian canceled an October weekend in which participants would pretend to be at the hotel during a murder and try to figure out who the killer was.

On July 1, 1994, Detective Tom Gilliam did a phone interview with a friend of Janet's mother. The woman, who lived in New Jersey, told the detective, that "I personally think she [Janet] knew who she was with" when she was killed.

Gilliam told her, "Well, we kinda felt that all along, maybe we don't know to what degree, but the fact that she was at least maybe possibly comfortable, at least comfortable enough to walk out on the beach with him."

On August 6, 1994, almost a year after the murder, Gilliam and Lieutenant Cliff Midgett reinterviewed Janet's brother Bob Siclari. He said he had a suspicious feeling that there was somebody waiting outside their hotel room door or nearby for Janet on the early morning when she was killed.

> *I kind of sensed that she was there with somebody. Because, you know, hey, you just get a sense about it. And I felt like if there was no one there she could have come in…brushed her hair, did something, you know, instead of in-and-out real quick and leaving everything in the room. I had a suspicious feeling that maybe somebody was waiting for her outside the door there or nearby.….She left the door ajar. It was open, and that is why I kind of thought somebody was there because it wasn't closed all the way, like you would if somebody was there and you wouldn't shut it in their face unnecessarily.*

Later that month, the investigators and Janet's family appealed to the public for help in solving the case. In a story in the *Coastland Times*, the family said they were putting up $18,000 of their own money for "information leading to the arrest and conviction of the perpetrator of

SBI Agent Donnie Varnell. *CNN's* Forensic Files *TV series*.

the crime." That money was in addition to $2,000 already pledged by the Dare County Crime Line.

Detective Gilliam kept working, In January 1995, he and a fellow detective went to Edison, New Jersey, and interviewed Janet's last boyfriend, Irshad Anderson. Janet's mother and a family friend told Gillian they suspected Anderson because he was a member of an outlaw motorcycle gang. In response to questioning, Anderson told the detectives that he had pulled five years in a Pennsylvania prison in connection with a gang-related homicide. He and Janet had been seeing each other off-again-on-again for five years because Anderson could not commit, but they "got along very well." Janet had asked him to go on the Outer Banks vacation with her, he said, but he declined because he didn't have the money.

Anderson voluntarily gave them a blood sample, the detectives said. The sample proved not a match to the semen found in Janet.

By 1997, Detective Gilliam and Donnie Varnell, a seasoned agent with the State Bureau of Investigation, were the lead investigators on the case.

7
THE DNA BREAKTHROUGH

On April 15, 1997, SBI Agent Mark Boodee, the DNA database manager for the SBI, found "a cold hit" matching the semen samples from Janet's case to a convicted offender. Such hits refer to suspects that have not previously been developed in a case.

By early 1997, the investigative team was at a dead end. Nags Head Police Detective Tom Gilliam and SBI Agent Donnie Varnell often consulted with Robert Trivette, their prosecutor friend who had been following the case since Gilliam had called him to the crime scene. "We were just throwing darts," Trivette later told the author.

Over almost four years, the investigators had done about three hundred interviews. They followed up on leads called into their department. They developed several suspects and then ruled them out. They contacted several TV shows trying to get media attention on the case. There was also a psychic, referred to the investigators by Janet's family. The investigators met with the psychic but gathered nothing useful for the case.

The investigators often studied photos of the crime scene, including that pair of high-top sneakers near the body. If they could only match those sneakers to their owner—and get a match on the semen found in Janet's body.

Since 1993, DNA testing had advanced greatly. Now there was a statewide database where DNA samples from crime scenes could be entered and compared with DNA samples taken from prisoners. The investigators on

Janet's case sent a semen sample to the base. On April 15, 1997, SBI Agent Mark Boodee, the database manager for the SBI, found "a cold hit" of the semen samples from Janet's case to a convicted offender. Such hits refer to suspects that have not been previously developed in a case.

Boodee let Mark Nelson, the SBI agent in charge of the molecular genetic section of the SBI lab, know. Nelson pulled the DNA database card and blood sample from the DNA repository. Nelson hand-carried the database card sample to Agent David Mishoe. Mishoe verified a match to a Thomas Jabin Berry. Boodee called the Nags Head team.

The investigators were thrilled. But they'd never heard of the prisoner whose DNA matched their sample, Thomas Jabin Berry. He had never been a suspect in the case until now, hence a "cold hit."

The investigators dove into learning all they could about Berry, who went by his middle name Jabin, finding that he was a thirty-one-year-old native of Engelhard, an old fishing village on the Pamlico Sound about thirty-five miles west of Nags Head. He'd worked as a commercial fisherman on seagoing boats and had also worked as a roofer. He'd been in trouble since his teenage years and was currently in the Columbus Correctional

Jabin Berry being led to a court appearance. *Drew C. Wilson.*

Institution at Whiteville, North Carolina, a drive of several hours south of Nags Head, where he was being held for violating probation on a 1992 conviction of taking indecent liberties with a minor, a twelve-year-old girl. He had received a ten-year sentence, suspended on the condition that he be on five years of supervised probation. His original charge had been sexual assault but had been plea-bargained to a charge of indecent liberties. He had violated his probation in 1995 by failing drug tests, causing his probation to be revoked. Had he not violated probation, his DNA would not have been entered into the state databank, as those DNA samples were not being entered into the state bank until the mid-1990s.

Robert Trivette, the assistant district attorney overseeing the Siclari case, had, as a new prosecutor, allowed Berry to take the plea bargain, a decision he later regretted. He was new to the job. He had aggressively pursued other sexual assault cases, he would later say, but he worried about putting a victim as young as Berry's on the witness stand. And there were indications from the victim's family, through a law enforcement officer close to them, that they wanted a plea bargain, Trivette said.

The investigators quickly made plans to visit Berry.

A SBI supervisor advised the investigators that Berry would deny killing Janet. They should be ready for that and get a warrant for a new blood test from him in hopes of getting a perfect DNA match.

Part II
The Reckoning

Northeastern North Carolina

8
CONFRONTING THOMAS JABIN BERRY

I don't remember her, I didn't have sex with her and I didn't kill her.
—Thomas Jabin Berry in his initial interview with investigators on May 9, 1997

On May 9, 1997, SBI Agent Donnie Varnell and Detective Tom Gilliam made the drive together from Nags Head to Whiteville to interview Jabin Berry. The investigators had decided that Varnell would take the lead role in the questioning since he had more experience investigating homicides than Gilliam. Varnell, who had begun his career with the police department in Wilson, North Carolina, and the sheriff's office there, had been involved in more than thirty homicide investigations since he'd joined the SBI. With Berry, Gilliam would play the "good cop," and Varnell, of medium height and build, easy with a smile but quick to go stone-faced, when need be, would play the "bad cop." Agent Mark Nelson of the SBI lab would sit in, ready to secure another blood sample from Berry when the time was right.

The Columbus Correctional Institution was the usual prison: bricks and barbed wire. A bailiff brought Berry to an interview room where the investigators sat waiting and unshackled him as the lawmen watched. Berry was brown-haired with a slight mustache and lazy green eyes, tattooed, five feet, nine inches tall, 145 pounds in his prison jumpsuit, quietly cocky. Like so many convicts, he was probably bored stiff inside, anxious for any outside contact. The lawmen talked Berry up, then read him his rights and got down to basics.

Varnell asked Berry about the conviction of taking indecent liberties with a minor.

"I had sex with her, but I didn't plead guilty to that," Berry told them. "I pled guilty to the lesser charge so I could get out of jail sooner."

Varnell soon turned the interview to Janet.

I don't remember her, I didn't have sex with her and I didn't kill her, Berry told them.

He was living in Engelhard in August 1993, he said, and rarely came north to the Outer Banks. When he did, he said, he visited his mother in Manteo, but he really couldn't remember. He would later say that around the weekend Janet was killed, he hitchhiked to Manteo to get an identification card at the NC Division of Motor Vehicles (DMV) office there. Such cards are issued as verification documents to those who lack driver's licenses.

The interview ended after an hour and forty-five minutes.

Agent Nelson secured the new blood sample. It soon came back a perfect match. DNA testing has varying degrees of certainty and challenges. For example, tests of hair roots produce better results than hair shafts, longer hairs beyond the roots. Of all DNA samples, semen/blood matches are among the most conclusive.

But getting a confession from Jabin Berry would prove hard. Though the DNA testing proved he'd had sex with Janet, the lawmen knew that Berry might contend his sex with Janet had been consensual, as outlandish as that was, a clean-living woman like Janet just hooking up with a rough stranger like Berry on the beach. The investigators had to prove Berry had raped and murdered Janet.

THE INVESTIGATORS GOT A boost on May 28, 1997, when Gilliam interviewed a former girlfriend of Berry's. Gilliam showed her the crime scene photo of the white tennis shoes. She studied the photo, recognizing the shoes.

"We had went out and bought a pair," she said. "I don't know if that's the exact same pair, but they were similar to those."

Gilliam asked her what size shoes Berry wore. Nine, she said. And he almost always wore gray socks, she said, like the ones stuffed in the shoes in the crime scene photo. The shoes found at the crime scene were size 9.

Gilliam must have been overjoyed, but he didn't show it. Berry might have left his shoes at the scene so as not to leave footprints. But if that was the case, his plan had backfired.

9
JABIN BERRY CRACKS

The Greenville SBI District Office
July 23, 1997

It looks like I was involved [in Janet's slaying], *I'm just not remembering it.*
—Jabin Berry in a July 23, 1997, interview with investigators.

On July 23, 1997, SBI Agent Donnie Varnell and Nags Head Police Detective Tom Gilliam did a second interview with Jabin Berry. They arranged to have Berry brought from the Elizabeth City prison to the SBI district office in Greenville, the same region of northeastern North Carolina as Nags Head.

The interview began about 6:10 p.m. in a large, rectangular meeting room with several tables. Department of Correction officers brought Berry in, took his handcuffs off and left.

As in the first interview, Varnell took the lead.

The investigators exchanged small talk with Berry: how you doing, how you been, etc. They gave him a soda and a cigarette, probably a Marlboro Light from Gilliam's pack, back in those days when he still smoked and smoking was still allowed in public buildings. Then they sat down at a table, Varnell on one side and Gilliam and Berry on the other side. They read Berry his Miranda rights, and he said he understood them and waived his right to counsel.

The investigators soon got into Janet's case. Berry told them, "I never met her, never had sex with her, didn't kill her and was not involved in her killing."

The investigators asked Berry about the ID card they'd secured from his mother's house in Manteo.

On August 27, 1993, Berry said, the day before Janet's body was found, he'd set out from Engelhard hitchhiking to the DMV office in Manteo to get the ID card. He brought his young child with him as he stood by US 264, his thumb out, searching for a ride. "It's hard for people not to stop when you have a child with you," he said.

Gilliam and Varnell must have thought: This man was not ashamed to use his little child, standing dangerously by the narrow shoulder of that highway, to help him hitchhike.

Berry caught a ride to Manteo, got the card and caught a ride back to Engelhard, bringing his child along, he said.

The next day, Berry said, or sometime around that, he was over on the beach, in the town of Kill Devil Hills at an oceanfront beach access near the 8 milepost, drinking and smoking crack with friends. "A cop ran us off because we were making too much noise," he said. He got a cab to Manteo, he said, but did not say where he went after that. "I was often all cracked out and f——— up then," he said.

The investigators showed him photos of Janet prior to her death and photos of her at the crime scene.

"I don't remember meeting her," Berry said.

The detectives kept pushing, asking Berry about what knives he might have had.

"I always carried a knife when I was not in prison," he said. "I had several different kinds of knives when I went to prison.…Around 1993, I had a sheaf knife with a gut hook on it."

Such knives have a hook on one side and a sharp edge on the other. Users plunge the point into fish or deer, then pull away from the hook to clean the game.

"I don't remember what happened to the sheaf knife, I think it was an Old Timer [brand]. I also had a 'sliming' knife, it was smaller, with a red handle and a serrated edge. I often used this type of knife working in fishing boats."

Such knives are used for gutting fish.

In response to further questioning from the detectives, Berry said he had never been to the Carolinian but had been to the bars at the Holiday Inn and Sea Ranch hotel in Kill Devil Hills.

Then Berry got into his troubled background. When he was about ten, he said, his father, drunk, was in bed with him and "started to hump him from behind and tried to stick his 'mess' into him." "He was calling my mama's name while he was doing this," Berry said. "I got away and ran to my grandmother's house and told her what happened. She didn't believe me, beat me and sent me back to my father's house. I never forgot that. I never forgot that. It affected me in a bad way and caused problems in later relationships. I wasn't there when my father died of cancer, and I've always been sorry for that. I still loved him."

Berry talked about an incestuous relationship with an aunt. "My family is kind of messed up that way. An aunt French-kissed me when I was about 13, saying I had the most kissable lips."

As a teenager, he said, he got in trouble for urinating behind an Engelhard store. Two girls saw his "mess," he said, and he was sent away to training school but ran away several times, resulting in him getting more time in training school.

As an adult, Berry told the investigators, he had an incident in Engelhard with a woman he described as his girlfriend. He broke a window at her house to get in to see her, he said, and when their visit "didn't work out" he ran from the house.

Later, he said, he was convicted of taking indecent liberties with the twelve-year-old in 1992 in Engelhard and sentenced to prison. He was twenty-five at the time. He told the detectives that he thought the girl was thirteen and the sex was consensual but now knew she was twelve—as if even thirteen would be consensual, which it would obviously not be.

Berry said he had no explanation as to why his semen was found in Janet's body. "It seems like you all have me, and if I was on a jury, I would think I was involved in her death. If I had raped and killed her, I don't remember it." He said words to that effect several times. "I would [have] had to be all f——— up on crack to have killed her," he said. "I would forget things when I was on crack, and I was smoking a lot of it in 1993....I would have had to be messed up on crack or really scared to kill somebody like that. It looks like I was involved, I'm just not remembering it."

That statement was a seismic shift. In the May interview, he'd said he didn't have sex with Janet and didn't kill her.

At one point, Varnell left the room to get Berry a hamburger from a nearby fast-food spot.

The investigators showed Berry photos of the high-top shoes found near Janet's body, with gray socks tucked into them. He wore shoes like that on fishing boats, he said, and wore gray socks most of the time. He didn't remember leaving his shoes on the Nags Head beach.

Then Berry said, "I might need a lawyer. I'm not sure I should be talking to you all."

Agent Varnell told Berry that was his choice, he wasn't being charged at this time, they just needed to know what really happened. Varnell told Berry he could get him a phonebook if he needed to call a lawyer.

Berry decided to continue to talk, according to Varnell.

"I love my children and want to see them again....I'll agree with you all that I have made some bad decisions in relationships with women," Berry said. "I have fought with women, women have hit me. That doesn't excuse me."

As he talked about his children, Berry's eyes teared up.

The investigators then asked: "If satellite photos had been shot of the crime scene, would they show you?"

Berry: "Probably. I do not remember killing her. From what I have heard, it sounds like I was involved. I would rather this be a manslaughter charge, if I had to make a choice." He had seen TV shows about those satellite photos, he said.

The investigators didn't tell Berry, but there were no satellite photos. They had been gaming him.

Berry didn't remember killing or raping Janet, he said, and didn't know how his semen had been found in her.

Varnell then made a play homicide investigators have long used to secure a confession: giving the suspect an "out." He asked Berry if he could have had consensual sex with Janet and "something went wrong." Berry said he didn't remember.

Berry was becoming "a little agitated," Varnell would later say.

Berry stood up. "I've got nothing else to say to you guys," he said. "I know you officers are just doing your jobs."

It was about 1:30 a.m., the interview having gone for almost seven and a half hours. The investigators knew that Berry had made incriminating statements. In their May interview with Berry at the Elizabeth City prison, he said he wasn't at the crime scene, he didn't rape or kill Janet. But in the latest interview, he had said: "For me to have done that, I would have to have been all f—— up and I don't remember."

The investigators must have realized that Berry was a ticking time bomb that exploded on Janet.

According to Berry's time frame, he had been partying at a Kill Devil Hills public beach access, about two miles north of the crime scene. But he had a relative who lived near the Carolinian. Maybe that landed him in Janet's orbit, whether he walked through a nearby public access, trespassed across someone's property or walked through the Carolinian parking lot. However he got there, it was part of the terrible confluence of circumstances that caused a woman who loved the sea to be slain within sight of her beloved water.

Records of the interview were based on Varnell's summary and later testimony from Varnell and Gilliam, as the interview was not tape-recorded or videotaped, which was not required by state law at the time, although tape recordings were often done across the state. The investigators on Janet's case taped several interviews with others.

The investigators already knew that Berry had tried to rape the woman in Engelhard, but for some reason, charges were never lodged against him. Regarding his twelve-year-old victim, his crime against her was, at the very least, sexual assault but had been plea-bargained to indecent liberties.

Soon after interviewing Jabin Berry, Gilliam and Varnell drove to Berry's hometown of Engelhard by the Pamlico Sound. It was a ride of almost an hour from Manteo, a hard left past Manns Harbor up US 264 West, a two-lane highway through thick swampland and spindly pines with little room by the road to pull over. It's a desolate ride, rolling past thousands of marshland acres that include a bombing range used by nearby air force and naval stations.

In warm months, it can be a beautiful ride down a road that some locals call "the butterfly highway" for the winged wonders along it. It's wild and rugged country, eloquently described by local author Charles Harry Whedbee in his book *Legends of the Outer Banks and Tar Heel Tidewater*:

> *The territory to the west of Roanoke Island was then, and remains today, some of the wildest and most inaccessible in this entire country of ours. Although there are settlements along the shorelines of the sounds and rivers, and although the adjacent waters are charted and familiar to many, the land mass remains largely as wild and unknown to man as the far side of the moon. Thousands upon thousands of acres remain upon which the foot of…man has never trod.…The area is as dangerous to the unwary visitor today as it was in the time of* [the Native American] *Manteo. You could step off one of those dirt roads and never be seen again. Bear are still there, rattlesnakes almost as big as a man's thigh,*

Top: Engelhard today. *Kathleen Railey*.

Bottom: Another shot of Engelhard today. *Kathleen Railey*.

Defendant Thomas Jabin Berry's hometown of Engelhard. *Kathleen Railey*.

as well as an assortment of wildcats. The practice bombs are supposed to be nonexplosive, but you could get yourself killed with a minimum of effort in that section.

Whedbee's book was published in 1966, several years before Jabin Berry was growing up in Engelhard. But during his formative years in the 1970s, the area was still a jungle unto itself, with an insular attitude wary of outsiders, especially of the law enforcement type, and so it was still as the investigators set out to interview Berry's kin and friends more than thirty years after Whedbee had set the scene, and so it remains today. "There's no law out here," one local told the author in 2023, a stretch, but not that far from the truth. As the investigators worked in 1997, locals quickly spread the word that the lawmen were there. But through interviews, the investigators established Berry's tough upbringing and his early descent into sexual assault crimes.

In addition to Berry's indecent liberties conviction, the investigators found other allegations of sex-related crimes against Berry. But for whatever reasons, charges had not been made.

In prison for the indecent liberties conviction, Berry had been labeled as a molester by fellow inmates. Gilliam interviewed one of those inmates, who said he had "two-picked" Berry, prison slang for hitting him with his right fist and following with his left.

BACK IN MANTEO, GILLIAM and Varnell interviewed Berry's mother, Doris M. Berry, at her home. She said she had a number of her son's belongings and brought them out to her living room for the detectives to go through. The investigators found the ID card Berry had mentioned getting in Manteo. The card was dated August 27, 1993—the day before Janet was killed. Berry's mother allowed them to take the card with them.

ON MARCH 30, 1998, a Dare County grand jury indicted Jabin Berry for the rape and first-degree murder of Janet.

Initial hearings were held at the courthouse in downtown Manteo. It's an old brick building with white pillars built in 1904, within sight of Shallowbag Bay, which elbows around the town waterfront and feeds into

The former courthouse in Manteo today where Jabin Berry was tried in 1999. *Author photo*.

the Roanoke Sound. Manteo is the seat of Dare County, just across the Sound from Nags Head.

Local attorneys John Graham and Mike Sanders were appointed to defend Berry, who was indigent. Berry pleaded not guilty at his arraignment. Both lawyers had grown up in nearby Elizabeth City and had gained wide

Engelhard recently. *Kathleen Railey*.

respect for their work. Graham, a surfer in his late thirties, a husband and father of two, had waited tables at the beach during his college years, including at the Carolinian. He'd secured his undergraduate degree from NC State University in Raleigh, then attained his law degree from the Walter F. George School of Law at Mercer University in Georgia. Graham

Jabin Berry's old Engelhard neighborhood. *Kathleen Railey*.

was lead counsel on the case, but he and Sanders, longtime friends, would work closely together as partners.

At a subsequent hearing, Assistant District Attorneys Robert Trivette and Amber Davis, star deputies in District Attorney Frank Parrish's office, announced that they would seek the death penalty against Berry. Davis had grown up on the Outer Banks, the daughter of Buddy Davis, a legendary boatbuilder. Trivette, who'd conferred with the investigators on the case from the start, is a native of Western North Carolina and had worked as a journalist, a high school teacher and a coach before earning a graduate degree in journalism from the University of North Carolina at Chapel Hill and a law degree there. He took a job as a prosecutor on the Outer Banks because he liked to fish.

The investigators kept working the case. In January 1998, they contacted the SBI lab to examine footprint impressions made by Jabin Berry for comparison with the footprints found at the crime scene. Detective Tom Gilliam and rookie Nags Head Police Officer Kevin Brinkley visited Jabin Berry in prison and collected the prints. The SBI testing on them was inconclusive. The lawmen then researched other ways of tying Berry to the crime scene. They found an expert, Sergeant Robert Kennedy with the Royal Canadian Mounted Police in Canada. Gilliam sent Kennedy forty-five to fifty photos of Berry's feet that he had taken with Brinkley.

For their part, Graham and Sanders, with some help from a private investigator, did much of their own investigating, including riding to their client's hometown of Engelhard and interviewing his friends and family.

Part III
THE TRIAL

10

"THE HORROR OF RANDOM CHANCE"

Janet happened to walk out on the beach at the wrong time, simple as that.
—*Assistant District Attorney Robert Trivette in his opening statement at Jabin Berry's trial*

Facing trial for their client in January 1999, defense attorneys John Graham and Mike Sanders had their backs against the wall, with the semen found in Janet a perfect match to their client's DNA and their client having talked himself deadly close to a confession. Attorneys in death penalty cases always hope for evidence that can lead to acquittals for their clients. But when that evidence is just not there, and they know their client could be killed by the state, the attorneys start a long dance with their clients, trying to persuade them that the evidence against them is concrete, their life is in danger and a plea bargain could save their lives, even if it means spending the rest of their lives behind bars. But the state wasn't offering a plea bargain to Berry, and he wouldn't be interested if they did. He was confident, even cocky, that he would be acquitted.

Once defendants make the decision to go for a trial—and it is the defendant's decision—defense lawyers buckle down, their only hope being that they can save their client's life.

The stakes were immense on both sides. This would be one of the first, if not the first, death penalty trial in Dare County. And it would be one of the first, if not the first, in which a defendant in the state in a capital murder case had been charged based on a cold DNA hit.

For the state and the defense, capital trials are all about storytelling, word wars over who controls the narrative that the jury will buy. The state tries to tell the victim's story in a way that will touch the hearts and souls of jurors, painting the defendant as a monster, just as the defense strives to tell their client's story, what he or she went through in childhood, to humanize them. And while, by law, the defendant is presumed innocent, that's not the case in the real world. In many capital trials, while the defense is under no obligation to point the finger at another suspect, good defense lawyers sometimes do that. That is what the defense would do in this case.

Graham and Nags Head Police Detective Tom Gilliam respected each other's work. Before the Siclari trial started, Graham and Gilliam had a meeting at Graham's law office to go over the evidence, with Graham telling Gilliam he would have to go at him hard in court, but that it was nothing personal, just part of the job in trying to save his client's life. Gilliam told Graham he understood, but if there was ever a poster boy for the needle, Jabin Berry was it.

For their part, the opposing lawyers were anticipating each other's moves: The prosecution figured the defense would seek to prove their client's sex

Berry on his way to court. *Drew C. Wilson.*

with the victim was consensual and that someone else killed her after that. The defense anticipated that the state would rely on the DNA evidence and argue that Berry's past crimes showed a course of conduct that led to the current charges. Trivette was confident that strategy would work, coupled with the DNA evidence.

The courtroom was packed as the trial began in the Manteo courthouse.

Bailiffs led the shackled Berry into the courtroom and then removed the chains as he took his seat by his lawyers in clothes lent to him by Sanders, an open-collared shirt and dress pants.

His dark hair was neatly trimmed and parted in the middle, and he had a slender mustache. He rarely smiled. He was on the small side, not nearly as foreboding as he might have liked to think he was. Sunbeams shone through the numerous tall windows in the courtroom, a bittersweet reminder to defendants that their freedom might be ebbing.

Judge Jerry Tillett, a Dare County native, former defense attorney and powerful force among local barristers, would be presiding.

After the usual lengthy jury selection for capital cases, the trial began.

This was the first death penalty trial for all the lawyers involved, friends cutting their teeth together in a capital trial. This was war. Short of Judge Tillett's rulings, it would be no holds barred, although friendships would continue outside the trial, in part because of shared experience that outsiders can't fathom, including endlessly studying photos of slain beauties, images that forever haunt.

Murder trials, even as they dwell on lives stolen, touch repeatedly on lives lived and are like weddings in that the defense sits at a table on one side, usually on the left side of the courtroom as one walks in, with their clients' family on wooden pews, at least in Manteo, right behind them. Prosecutors use a table to the right of the courtroom with the victim's family behind them. Detective Gilliam and Agent Donnie Varnell sat right behind them, ready to give whispered assistance as needed.

Assistant DA Robert Trivette, tall and somberly slim, led off with his opening statement, setting the eerie summer night scene of six years before, a brilliantly imagined scenario based on the evidence. The image he'd seen of Janet's body on the beach almost six years ago was still on his brain, fueling his drive to convict Jabin Berry.

> Judge Tillett, Mr. Graham, Mr. Sanders, ladies and gentlemen of the jury, it was a warm summer night, a woman is out on the beach alone. It's dark out there.

It's toward the end of the season, just a few days before Labor Day, the last week of August 1993. This woman is out listening to the ocean, smelling the ocean one last time before she returns in the morning to her job and her life in New Jersey. She loves the ocean. It is her favorite spot on the earth, and she is there in the middle of the night only a few hours before sunrise because she loves the ocean.

Behind her in a hotel not more than 100 yards away, her brother is asleep and two of her friends are asleep, and in just a few minutes she will return to that room where she is staying with them, get up the next day and return home.

Perhaps as she starts back, perhaps from behind her, perhaps from the side, but out of the darkness, a man suddenly approaches her. He startles her but she is not immediately afraid for herself or her person because she is a confident woman. She is 35 years old. She is a trusting person who believes in the goodness of other human beings, and she is a beautiful woman who all her life has had men to come to her and approach her and she has always been able to handle these situations.

But on this night, this early morning hour, her trust in human nature lets her down and the man comes quickly to her, perhaps, and grabs her and suddenly there is a knife, and that knife is at her throat. And suddenly the panic in her stomach rises into her chest and into her heart. The point of the knife is at her throat, and it pierces her skin as he demands of her to take her clothes off. She has on a pair of shorts. And her mind begins to rush as she tries to remember what she is supposed to do in this situation. Again, the point of the knife is right there under her chin and the blood begins to trickle out. Her mind swirls and she stalls for time, taking her belt off, but she complies with the man.

Suddenly she's down on the ground and there's a sharp pain across her throat as she begins to go limp now. She doesn't—she can't move. He has got her by her hands. He is bigger than she is. He weighs more than she does. And that knife is still at her throat.

Suddenly she now realizes that he is inside her and she tries to throw up but there is nothing in her stomach. He finishes with her. Again, the knife is still at her throat, and she can't move and she is not sure where he is but he still has her and there's suddenly a sharper and deeper pain over on the left side of her throat and her head spins and she almost loses consciousness and she realizes now that she is in big trouble because she is seriously hurt. She also realizes the man is gone. She tries to scream, and she opens her mouth and nothing comes out, no sound, no noise, no scream, not even a whisper. And she knows now her front is covered with blood and she must do something to save herself.

So she tries to stand up but she becomes dizzy and light-headed and is only able to move a few feet and then her legs buckle underneath her. And she tries to scream again, and she can't and she doesn't understand why. She is breathing, she can feel her lungs moving but it's like there's no air going in. In fact, when she breathes, what it feels like is that there's fluid filling up her lungs.

And she crumples now in a kneeling position, in a sitting position. The blood is covering her front and she takes her pants, her shorts, which are off, and she pushes them against the hole in her jugular vein where she is bleeding to death. And then Janet Siclari slumps over on her left shoulder clutching those shorts to her neck. She pulls her knees up in a fetal position into a ball, drifts off into unconsciousness and dies in a pool of her own blood.

Ladies and gentlemen, Jabin Berry raped and murdered Janet Siclari on the beach in front of the Carolinian hotel a few hours before sunrise on August 28, 1993. She died as a result of one specific cut to her throat, a knife that penetrated the left side of her throat. Dr. Page Hudson, the doctor, medical pathologist, who performed the autopsy on her will tell you that cut severed her left jugular vein, cutting it almost completely in half. That same knife blow also severed her larynx, causing her not to be able to speak, to scream, to whisper, to say a word.

When she breathed after that knife blow, that blood also ran out of her body, ran down her windpipe out of her lungs, almost filling up her left lung....In addition to the cuts that we found on Janet Siclari's body, we also found inside of her vagina, sperm, male spermatozoa. That was collected by Dr. Page Hudson when he performed the autopsy. It was sent to the SBI where it was transferred into a DNA sample. Later on, it was compared to a blood sample taken out of the arm of Jabin Berry. The blood sample taken out of the arm of Jabin Berry was a perfect DNA match to the semen recovered out of the vagina of Janet Siclari.

How did these two end up on the beach that morning, those few hours before sunrise in August of 1993? I can't tell you much about how Jabin Berry got there. When he was interviewed by the Nags Head Police Department and the SBI later, he told them he was not there, that he did not kill Janet Siclari, that he did not rape her and that he did not know her. He said that in one interview. In another subsequent interview, he said he did not remember killing Janet Siclari, and no, he did not have an answer for why his semen was inside of Janet Siclari.

How did Janet Siclari end up there? How did she cross paths with Jabin Berry? This is the horror that we all think about in the back of our minds, this is the horror of random chance. She happened to walk out on the beach at the wrong time, simple as that. She did not know Jabin Berry. She had never come across him in her life. She had never seen him. She had never met him.

She was a 35-year-old single woman from North Arlington, New Jersey who was on vacation here that week. She was petite. She was beautiful. She was 95 pounds on the night she died. In her bare feet, she did not stand five feet tall. She worked as an ultrasound technician in a hospital in Passaic, New Jersey, where she had been for almost 10 years....

The ocean was Janet Siclari's weakness. She loved to be at the beach and any opportunity she had she would go there. And it's so terribly ironic because you could say in a way that it was her love that got her killed. It caused her to stay that extra day at the Outer Banks and it caused her to walk out on the beach that last night, that last time to see it one more time. The next morning, she was supposed to return to New Jersey and go back to her work and her job....

Ladies and gentlemen, Jabin Berry raped and murdered Janet Siclari on the beach in front of the hotel in August 1993....At the end of this trial, I will stand back up here and ask you to convict him of the crimes he has committed, the murder and rape of Janet Siclari. Thank you.

11
MATLOCK ENTERS THE COURTROOM

Then, in a scene straight out of Matlock, *the popular TV show of the 1990s starring Manteo's own Andy Griffith as a fictional defense attorney, real-life defense attorney John Graham pointed the finger at Randy Powers, the Carolinian bartender whom Janet had given a ride home in her last hours.*

Defense attorney John Graham fixed his earnest eyes on the jurors and began his opening statement. Graham is inherently likeable in an ageless, boy-like way and exudes honesty. Graham, who'd once worked at the Carolinian, set the scene, telling jurors that that the old hotel "would factor very importantly into this case." Then the attorney, as hard as it might have been for him, suggested that Janet's sex with his client may have been consensual. You do what you have to do in a death penalty case, trying to save your client's life, as a North Carolina capital defense attorney recently said.

Graham said:

> We believe, at the conclusion of the state's evidence, they will have proved two things beyond a reasonable doubt to you. The first thing is that their test results indicate a DNA match between the semen found in her body and Jabin Berry. And the second thing they will prove is, obviously, she was murdered. What the state will not be able to prove to you and what you need to look at when you listen to the

Berry in court with his lawyers, *left to right*: Mike Sanders, John Graham and Berry. *Drew C. Wilson.*

facts of this case—listen to evidence concerning a link, a chain or connection between the DNA test results and the murder of Janet Siclari. And we believe after you hear the evidence there are going to be a number of very troubling questions that have been raised by evidence presented to you that are going to compel you to come back with a verdict of not guilty....

DNA goes to the issue of identification. DNA cannot and does not go to the issue of consent or lack of consent on behalf of the victim.

In other words, Jabin Berry might well have had sex with Janet, but that sex may have been consensual. Berry left after that and someone else killed Janet.

Continuing that theory, in a scene straight out of *Matlock*, the popular TV show of the 1990s starring Manteo's own Andy Griffith as a defense attorney, Graham pointed the finger at Randy Powers, the Carolinian bartender whom Janet had given a ride home in her last hours. Graham detailed that Powers had then driven back to the Carolinian, sitting in his friend's car, slicing a stick of pepperoni with a knife while waiting for his girlfriend, then drove his friend's car back to his nearby cottage and walked back to the Carolinian parking lot, still looking for his girlfriend, Faith Hopkins:

> So Randy Powers then walks back down to the Carolinian and is in the process of attempting to break into Faith Hopkins' room when Faith Hopkins drives up. He approaches her, he has a confrontation, he slaps her and then Randy Powers stalks off.
>
> The evidence will be that Faith Hopkins was almost identical physically, hair color, as well as even the clothes she was wearing that night, the color, all the way down to the color of her shorts [to Janet's]. So you need to listen to that evidence.

Graham noted to the jurors that the investigators' interrogation of Jabin Berry in Greenville in 1997 was not audiotaped or videotaped, "unlike almost every other interview that was done in this case."

Graham closed:

> I feel like if you can't answer these questions that this evidence is going to raise at the close of this case, then you will have no other choice but to return a verdict of not guilty, and that is what we are going to ask you to do. Thank you very much.

So Berry's lawyers would not be presenting an alibi defense, presenting witnesses to say their client couldn't have been at the crime scene. Instead, their strategy would be to poke holes in the state's case and point the finger at another suspect. It was all the defense could do, but it was risky. If the jury convicted their client, they might well go into the sentencing phase with the jury angry at him.

THE STATE BEGAN ITS case with the testimony of Vincent Lamont Freeman, the employee of the Nags Head Public Works Department who came upon Janet's body on the beach.

Soon thereafter, the state called to the stand Randy Powers, the Carolinian bartender. Originally a suspect in the case, then cleared, he was not subpoenaed, but was in court of his own accord. Assistant DA Amber Davis led him through his testimony, a basic recounting of what he had told the investigators, including that he had taken a knife from his kitchen and a stick of pepperoni before heading back to the Carolinian in the early morning hours before Janet's body was found.

On cross-examination, defense attorney Mike Sanders went hard at Powers, subtly suggesting that Powers might be a suspect in Janet's slaying by his aggressive actions that night, going at the former army soldier on his interactions with his girlfriend, Faith Hopkins.

Sanders	And she danced with someone and after the dance you gave this man what you called a, quote, "a little warning"?
Powers	Correct.
Sanders	Tell the jury what that means.
Powers	I grabbed his wrist that was resting on her rear end, grabbed it tightly and told him to keep off of it.
Sanders	Is that all you said or did you make any sort of a threat to do harm to him?
Powers	I very well could have. I don't recall exactly what was said. I was a little hot at that point.

On redirect examination, Assistant DA Davis questioned Powers about the knife he had brought to the Carolinian.

Davis	When you took the knife, did you intend to do anything with the knife other than cut pepperoni?
Powers	No.
Davis	Did you ever use that knife for anything other than cutting pepperoni?
Powers	Other than using it at the house, no.

Davis continued, asking Powers if he ever went out on the beach where Janet's body was found when he returned to the Carolinian, seeking his girlfriend. He did not go out on the beach, Powers testified, and in response to another question from Davis, he said he did not attack Janet on the beach.

THE STATE THEN CALLED Mark Boodee, the SBI's DNA expert, to the stand. Boodee could take the then-emerging DNA science and explain it in layman's language:

ADA Davis	Is it your opinion, Mr. Boodee, that the semen that was found from the vaginal swabs inside Janet Siclari came from Jabin Berry?
Boodee	In my opinion, it is scientifically unreasonable that it could have come from anyone other than the defendant, including a close relative.

Defense attorney John Graham gamely tried to question Boodee's findings, but they were airtight.

Davis then called Berry's former girlfriend, who had talked to Detective Tom Gilliam about Berry's shoes. She repeated what she'd told Detective Gilliam: that she'd been with Berry when he bought a pair of sneakers that looked almost like the ones in the crime scene photo, that he wore the same size, 9, as those sneakers, and that he almost always wore gray socks, like the ones found at the crime scene stuffed inside the sneakers.

Next, Davis called another former love interest of Berry to the stand. About "98 percent of the time" when they were together, she said, Berry wore a sheaf knife.

DAVIS AND TRIVETTE ARGUED before Judge Tillett, with the jury out of the courtroom, that Mary Smith should be called to the stand. Berry had sexually assaulted Smith in the summer of 1992, when she was in her twenties. Through Smith's testimony, the prosecution wanted to establish a course of conduct for the jury to see that led to Berry killing Janet.

With the jury out of the courtroom, Smith testified that she had lived near Berry in Engelhard.

Davis, in her questioning, then walked Smith through a traumatic night.

Davis	I'm going to turn your attention to a night when you were home alone. Did you ever have anything unusual occur between you and Mr. Berry on a night when you were home by yourself?
Smith	He knocked on my door one morning around 3 o'clock in the morning and I told him to go away and went back to bed. And the next thing I knew, he had took his pants off and jumped on me and snatched my underpants off and was trying to penetrate me.…He was bleeding from his arm where he had broken into the window, cut his arm…a lot of blood…going everywhere.

In response to further questioning, Smith testified that it had been about ten minutes between Berry's knock and his assault on her. He cut on the light in her bedroom, she told the court.

Smith	He was bleeding and trying to do whatever and I just said, you know, "I will do whatever you want, just let me take care of your arm first." His arm was cut real bad.
Davis	Why did you do that?
Smith	So I could get away from him.

Smith said she went into her kitchen, ostensibly to get paper towels to apply to Berry's bleeding arm, but pulled on some clothes and fled to a friend's house.

On cross-examination by defense attorney Graham, Smith acknowledged that she talked to a deputy from Hyde County, which borders Dare County and includes Engelhard, but did not pursue sexual assault charges against Berry.

Defense attorney Graham fought back: "When you just look at the pure facts, Judge Tillett, their theory of [Janet's] case is that this was a random act."

Smith knew Berry, Graham noted. Graham argued that Berry "went into a house versus an incident that occurred on the beach":

And then, obviously Judge, when [Smith] woke up and saw him and got out, he backed off and doesn't pursue her anymore, unlike what their theory is on the beach.

To further buttress the state's case against Berry on a course of conduct leading to Janet's slaying, the state argued before Judge Tillett, with the jury still out, to admit the testimony of Susan Jones, another of Berry's sexual assault victims.

Davis	And in this particular case [that of Janet], one of the motives for killing her was, number one—or one of the motives for using the knife was to keep her from running. He felt it necessary based on the fact that he had done that previously.

Trivette led Jones, a nineteen-year-old, through her testimony. He expertly guided her through what Berry had done to her when she was in middle school. Trivette started with a flourish sure to appeal to the judge's sympathy to get in the testimony of Jones.

Trivette	Susan, can see your mama back there [in the courtroom]?
Jones	Yes sir.
Trivette	You got to talk so she can hear you, OK?
Jones	OK.

Trivette took the witness back to the winter of 1992, when she was twelve years old. Trivette gently led Jones to Berry's assault on her.

Jones	He came over to my house and we were—I was being babysitted by my brother's girlfriend and he [Berry] and we were laying on the bed, all three of us in my mom's room and he tried to go up in my pants.

Jones said she pushed Berry away, and he got up and left.

Then, she testified, in the early spring of 1992, on the pretext of looking for a missing nephew in the Engelhard woods, Berry again assaulted her. He pushed her to the ground and climbed on top of her, she said, and pulled her pants off and one leg of her underpants. Then, she testified, he raped her. "He told me not to scream or yell or he would hurt me and my family, me and my mom," Jones told the court. "He told me if I told he would kill me or my mom."

She didn't tell her mother because she was scared, Jones testified, but she eventually told a friend.

A charge of sexual assault was brought against Berry, but his lawyer plea-bargained that to a conviction of taking indecent liberties with a minor child. Berry got a suspended sentence but landed in prison after violating his probation. That was the case that Trivette had, to his regret, allowed Berry to enter a plea in for reasons including that there were indications from the victim's family, through a law enforcement officer close to them, that they wanted a plea bargain, Trivette told the author.

In arguing for the inclusion of the Smith and Jones testimony, Trivette told Judge Tillett that the testimony went to Berry's course of conduct. Berry "did not want to leave another victim around that could cause trouble for him," Trivette argued.

The defense fought hard against the entry of the testimony of Smith and Jones, but Tillett allowed it. The jury heard it.

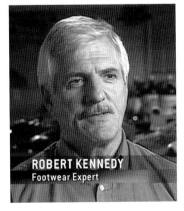

Robert Kennedy of the Royal Canadian Mounted Police, who presented footprint testimony at Jabin Berry's trial. *CNN's* Forensic Files *TV series.*

NEXT, TRIVETTE CALLED TO the stand the Royal Canadian Mounted Police Officer Sergeant Robert Kennedy, whom the investigators had interviewed about Berry's footprints. Kennedy, from Ottawa, testified that he had worked for twenty-seven years with his agency's forensic identification unit.

Kenney had compared the footprint impressions the investigators made in prison of Berry to the pair of tennis shoes found at the crime scene. "I found no dissimilarities that would cause me to think somebody else wore the shoes," Kennedy testified.

The defense rigorously challenged Kennedy's science.

The state rested. The defense called no witnesses.

12

SPEAKING FOR JANET

One in 112 trillion. Those are the chances that anyone, that is the chance that anyone other than this man, the defendant, Jabin Berry, left that DNA there in Janet Siclari.
—Assistant DA Amber Davis in her closing argument

Assistant DA Amber Davis began the state's closing arguments. She is a native Roanoke Islander, the daughter of Buddy Davis, a legendary Dare County builder of sportfishing boats who had started his career as a charter boat captain. Amber Davis knew well how to reach the local jury. She began her argument:

> On August 28th of 1993, it was the early morning hours there on the beach, and this man, the defendant Thomas Jabin Berry, raped and then brutally killed Janet Siclari there on the beach that morning. And unfortunately, like happens in most murder cases, we talk a lot about the defendant, but we don't know that much about the victim, Janet Siclari. She is dead. She has been dead since 1993, and she will never have the opportunity to come in here to court and tell you what happened. So let's talk about Janet and what we know about her.
>
> We know that she was an attractive, vivacious, compassionate young woman. She was thirty-something

years old. She was down here with friends trying to relax and have a good time and just hang out. They were in Southern Shores and, you know, things have changed a lot in a few years….Southern Shores wasn't really that happening of a place in '93, there wasn't a lot going on. She was up there to get away from the rat race…to come down here and have some peace and quiet.

Davis noted that Janet, her brother and their friends had "hung out as a group":

Let's look at this group. It consisted of Janet. She was a young medical technician, did ultrasounds for a hospital in New Jersey. She was with her brother.…She was with her friend Nora, an engineer since she got out of college. She was with Carrie Purvis who was in advertising.…This was a group of young thirty-something professionals down here to get away from the city and get away from the rat race and enjoy the peace and quiet that the Outer Banks has to offer. They came here to get away. They didn't come here to party and sow their wild oats and do stupid things like we see college kids do. They came here to enjoy each other and to get away.…

So they hung out and then [Friday night at the Carolinian] they do what they have done the whole week, they go to dinner as a whole group.…And Janet and the girls weren't ready to call it quits yet, you know, it's their vacation and it's the end and they just don't want to throw in the towel and deal with reality and think about going back to the rat race.

So they say, well you know, somebody mentioned the Port O' Call, I think Randy Powers and some of the other guys are going there, maybe we'll slip up there. And Bob…he is tired, really doesn't want to go out so he tells them, you know, "Go out and I'll just go on and go to bed."

And they do. They find a teller machine and they go on over to the Port O' Call. And it's a typical bar on a summer night, people dancing, people coming and going. They have a couple of drinks. But unfortunately, Nora Martin and Carrie Purvis had just given out. The day had just worn them out and they were tired, ready to throw in the towel and go home. But Janet, as always, she was vivacious and she just didn't want to deal with reality: "Let me stay an hour or so longer. Randy Powers is here, along with a couple of the other friends we met at the Carolinian. There are people I'm comfortable here with. I am only just a few minutes' drive from the Carolinian, I can make it back by myself, don't worry about me, go on without me."…

And Janet stays there and dances with a guy, Randy Powers says he's kind of goofy looking, but she dances with him, and she talks with Randy and their friends. And then it's last call and the lights come on and she's kind of trying to lose this goofy guy that's dancing with her. She doesn't want to be rude. She doesn't want to hurt his feelings but she definitely doesn't want to go home with him, she's not interested in hooking up with somebody. So she tells Randy, "Hey let me give you a ride home, I'll give you a ride home." You know, Randy had a lot going on, his girlfriend had just blown him off, she's dancing with a guy, the guy is hanging all over her, and it happens. It's a common scene at a bar on the beach in the middle of the summer. It's happened to some of us, I'm sure. We've had that happen. We've had those domestic situations occur, and he is preoccupied but not so much that he doesn't realize that Janet is trying to shake this guy. So he says, "Sure you can give me a ride home."

And they ride home, five minutes maybe at the most… and Randy gets out of the car, you know, "Bye, thanks, have a great trip back to New Jersey, take care of yourself." And he watches Janet drive off and obviously somewhere along the way she decided she needed a pack of cigarettes or maybe some aspirin or maybe something to drink. So she goes to a convenience store. We don't know where she went. We don't know for a fact she went to a convenience store. We do know she had a new pack of cigarettes and it's a pretty reasonable assumption. She wasn't gone very long and the closest store at the time was probably the 7-Eleven [on the bypass in Kill Devil Hills, about a mile north of the Carolinian].

Randy goes on into [his] house and he's still aggravated with Faith and he wants to have it out, you know, is she still going to leave, is she going to hook up with somebody else, what is the deal with that, why is she blowing me off? So he goes in the house, it's after 2 o'clock in the morning, and he is hungry, and he grabs a stick of pepperoni and a steak knife and he heads on down to the Carolinian in his roommate's car. And while he is sitting there in the parking lot waiting for Faith, he sees a car pulling in and he looks at the car and, at first, he thinks it's Faith and when the person gets out and she gets closer he realizes it's Janet. They don't look that much alike that he's going to mistake them up close. He realizes it's Janet, she's a lot smaller, she's four feet, eleven. Faith is about five-four and heavier. And he realizes it's Janet and sees her walk into the hotel by herself.

Well, when Nora said that she and Carrie walked into the hotel that night and there was nobody at the front desk, Randy indicated it certainly wasn't unusual at that time for there to be nobody at the front desk. And [Janet] walks on in and heads towards her room, rattles her keys and she gets in and Robert has probably been asleep for a couple of hours. And he hears the door and he sits up, he's tired, he knows he has to drive to New Jersey the next day and he sees it's his sister. And Janet comes in and she says, "It's only me." And she kicks her shoes off and lights the cigarette and he watches her lay the match down. And then she heads out of the room.

Now, sure, Robert told the police that he got the sensation that somebody was [outside their room]. But he has done a lot of soul searching and he has tried to remember as best he can what happened that night. But he never remembers Janet speaking to anyone other than him. He never remembers seeing anyone other than Janet and he never remembers hearing anyone speak to Janet. The TV was going on and in his mind, he is expecting and truly believes that Janet was with the girls that night when she came in. You know, it's kind of one of those dreams that's half mixed with reality and he's tried and tried to remember. And he's told the police everything he can absolutely remember. But the bottom line is, he didn't see or hear anyone.

Janet heads on out and she heads down to the beach and she sits down and smokes her cigarette, just enjoying peace and quiet. And unfortunately for Janet, that is when her path crossed with the defendant, Thomas Jabin Berry.

Before we go into detail about what happened, let's ask, "What do we know about the defendant?" We know a little about Janet, but what do we know about the defendant, Thomas Berry? Well, we know at this time in August of 1993 that he had the motive, he had the opportunity, and he had the ability to rape and kill Janet Siclari.

So what am I talking about? Well. let's talk about motive. In August of 1993 and during the previous year, the defendant was engaged in what we legally refer to as a common plan or scheme. He had a modus operandi, a mode of operation where he sexually assaulted young women.…

So he had a motive to kill Janet Siclari. She fought with him. She resisted him and he knew that Janet Siclari would report him to the police, and he knew that there was no way he was going back to jail again. So he had the motive. He was the one person that night who had the motive to rape Janet Siclari and he had the motive to kill Janet Siclari.

He also had the opportunity. One in 112 trillion [from the SBI expert]. Those are the chances that anyone, that is the chance that anyone other than this man, the defendant, Jabin Berry, left that DNA there in Janet Siclari.…

So what happened that particular night?…

I would submit to you that Janet is sitting there on the beach and she's enjoying the peace and quiet and all of a sudden she looks up and there's a strange man. And he comes up and he's kind of rough-looking and he makes her a little bit uncomfortable, gives her the willies and she's thinking, "Well, gee, maybe I better head on back to the hotel because this guy, there is something that is just not right about him." And she's there on the beach in the middle of the night and a strange guy approaches her. But she's compassionate and she's nice and she certainly doesn't want anybody to think that she's stuck-up. And he says something to her and she speaks, not wanting to offend him, but she's going to head on back to the hotel.

And when she turns to head back to the hotel, something goes terribly, terribly wrong. The defendant grabs her and he tries to take her pants off and she's like "Wait a minute, just wait a minute. If you just let go of me I'll do whatever you ask." Just like Mary Smith: "I will do whatever you ask, just let go of me." And he does. And maybe she tries to run, we don't know. But we do know that at some point a knife presented itself. And we know that a knife was used on Janet Siclari.

And I'd submit to you that at that point Janet does exactly what the defendant tells her to do. She takes her pants off. He doesn't care about her shirt, he wants her pants off. First she takes her belt off, loop by loop, taking her belt out. She is thinking "Maybe I can use this for a weapon, dear God, if I stall, if I stall, maybe he won't kill me."…But she takes her belt off. Not something you do when you're having consensual sex. It's something you do when you are stalling. And she takes her belt off and then she takes her pants off and then he tells her to take her underwear off and she does it. There's a knife in her face so she does it.

And she's talking to him and she has her underwear and her pants in her hand and she's talking to him, trying to talk him out of it. And she's not even thinking and she's doing stuff with her hands and she's winding her belt up, stuffing her underwear in her pockets, keeping her hands busy and her mind is racing.….

Then he pushes her down on the sand [and rapes her.]… And he's laying there and he knows at that point he has to kill Janet Siclari. He knows that she's going to report him if he leaves her alive. He knows he is on probation and he cannot go back to jail again. No woman is worth going back to jail for.…

And at that point he makes the premeditated and deliberate decision. He slices at her throat. And Janet feels that pain and she says, hey, this is different from the other. He is not poking me with a knife now and forcing me to do something, this guy is trying to kill me. And she knew he was trying to kill her. And at that point she fought with everything that her 95-pound body would allow her to fight with. But, you know, 95 pounds just doesn't do a lot when you are up against somebody like Jabin Berry. He is not large either, but he had a knife and held her down and he sliced at her again and this time it was a serious slice and blood was everywhere and Janet goes limp.

And he runs. He runs, leaving her there to die, hoping she is going to die because he sure as heck doesn't want her reporting him. And he runs and Janet lays there and grabs for her shorts. She's got medical experience and she is thinking "If I can just stop the bleeding maybe I can make it back to the hotel, maybe I am not cut that badly." But at the same time blood is running into her lungs and she can taste the blood as it's in her throat. And she knows, she knows that she is dying. And she tries to head toward the steps and she stumbles toward the steps and she just runs out of energy, she just cannot make it.

And she stumbles to her knees and she lays there and she knows she is dying and, as Dr. Hudson said, she had several minutes where she was conscious. She had several minutes where she laid there and she has thoughts racing through her mind like, "My mama, my mama is not going to know what happened to me. I am never going to see my mama again." She has those thoughts going through her mind and her brother is not going to know what happened to her and oh, dear God, what are my friends going to think when they wake up in the morning and all of her dreams for the future are gone.

Davis held back tears as she continued.

This man took her life away. And slowly her pulse weakens, her heart stops and she lays there and bleeds to death and the next morning the garbagemen find her, ladies and gentlemen. The garbagemen find Janet Siclari half-nude laying on the beach. They find her there just like a piece of trash where the defendant, Thomas Jabin Berry, left her, left her to die just like a piece of garbage. And they find her there, ladies and gentlemen.

Thomas Jabin Berry raped and killed Janet Siclari that night on the beach, there's no doubt about that. [The SBI] said that it's scientifically unreasonable to believe that anyone other than the defendant left that semen there on the beach, left that semen in Janet Siclari that night. Well, likewise, it's absolutely unreasonable to believe that Janet Siclari, a bright, attractive, young professional woman would engage in consensual sex with the likes of Thomas Jabin Berry. It's absolutely unreasonable to believe that.

The defense is going to argue to you, hey, you don't know it wasn't consensual sex. Well, let me tell you, every piece of evidence that came from that witness stand, every piece of evidence that you saw and heard suggests that the sex that night was nonconsensual. Plain and simply, she was raped that night, ladies and gentlemen.

So how do we know that it was rape? How do we know that the sex was nonconsensual? Well first of all you have the compliance wounds. What did Dr. Hudson tell you about those wounds? He said that they are common, that they are associated with using a knife or using a weapon to threaten someone, or to force them to comply, to put them into submission. And he was asked about those wounds and said based on the number of those wounds, in his opinion, they were compliance wounds.

You have defensive wounds. You know that Janet Siclari fought her attacker. There were wounds on her hands, there were some pretty big gouges there. And you can imagine what it is like to grab a knife when somebody is trying to kill you. He said, based on the location of the wounds, when asked, he said she was probably sliced at or grabbed at the knife more than one time.

So you have defensive wounds. And it's obvious that Janet Siclari went down fighting with as much fight as her 95-pound body could muster.

And you know the defense is going to say, well, they asked Dr. Hudson, did she have any vaginal trauma? No, she doesn't have any vaginal trauma. And they are going to say, well, no vaginal trauma, no sexual assault. That is wrong, ladies and gentlemen, that is absolutely wrong. Dr. Hudson told you it was not unusual at all…for there to be no vaginal trauma in sexual assault cases.…

She certainly is not Jabin Berry's type. And if [Janet] was dying to hook up with somebody, I would submit to you that there were a lot of young men at the Port O' Call that night she could have hooked up with. It is absolutely unreasonable to believe that she walked out on the beach and had consensual sex with Jabin Berry within an hour or so, period, when she was unaccounted for. Absolutely unreasonable to believe that.

What else is absolutely unreasonable? What about Randy Powers? The defense would love for you to believe that Randy Powers just jumped out there out of the sand dunes, out of the sea oats, and slit Janet Siclari's throat. They would love for you to believe that, they'd love for you to think it was a case of mistaken identity and that he killed Janet when he was mad at Faith. But does that make sense, ladies and gentlemen? Does that really make sense to you?…

What about Randy Powers? Randy told the good with the bad. He came down here voluntarily. He testified for you voluntarily without a subpoena. He was in Virginia. We could never have forced him to come down here without a long, lengthy process. And he came down here voluntarily. He went to the police voluntarily that morning when he found out that Janet was dead. He went to the police. And do you know what it's like to have to go to the police and say, hey, I was probably the last person that was seen with this woman?

That is not a pleasant thing to have to do. And he went to the police and he did that and he told them every negative thing you heard on the witness stand and everything that you—that they cross-examined him about. He told the police himself. He told them he had a knife. He told them about the pepperoni. He told them he was mad as heck at Faith and he was sitting there in the parking lot waiting for Faith. Sure, he was staking Faith out, waiting on her. He was going to fight with her and have it out with her. But that doesn't mean he killed Janet Siclari. That is absolutely unreasonable for you to believe otherwise.

We also know that Randy's DNA was not in Janet and we know way before 1997 he was eliminated as a suspect. Sure, he was probably one of the very first people that Tom Gilliam and those detectives zeroed in on. He was one of the last people to see her alive. So sure, they zeroed in on him but he gave blood, he gave hair and he did numerous other tests. And these guys over here [the investigators], they interviewed 200 to 300 people. You can rest assured they interviewed everyone who knew anything about Randy Powers' comings and goings that night. And you can rest assured that if that didn't check out they would have done a heck of a lot more. Randy Powers is not the person who killed Janet Siclari.

Davis cautioned the jurors not to buy into what the defense would likely contend in its closing arguments. "They are going to try to put up a smokescreen because the last person they want you focusing on is the defendant, Thomas Jabin Berry," she said in closing.

It was a powerful argument, leaving jurors spellbound. One thing the boatbuilder's daughter did not mention: Among commercial fishermen who live and sometimes die by the shipmates they work with, Jabin Berry was not known to be a steady hand to have his mates' backs on the deadly waters. They didn't like him or trust him.

13
THE DEFENSE GUNS THE STATE'S CASE

In his closing argument, Assistant District Attorney Robert Trivette followed up on ADA Amber Davis. He noted that the state legislature established the DNA database in 1993, "the computer network system that attempts to match offender blood against unsolved cases." Janet's DNA was entered into the system in 1994, he said, after the system "was up and running." There was a backlog, he said, but they finally got the "cold hit" on Berry in the spring of 1997. He talked about the absolute scientific certainty through the DNA testing that the semen found in Janet was Berry's and anticipated that the defense would argue, as "their only hope," that his sex with Janet was consensual.

Trivette mentioned the testimony from the Royal Canadian Mounted Police officer on Berry's footprints and his shoes, acknowledging that it was not "a perfect science" but that the officer said it was "likely" that Berry wore the shoes found at the crime scene.

Trivette noted that Berry, under investigators' questioning, had no explanation as to how his semen was found in Janet's body.

Janet, Trivette said, "was executed....She was executed to eliminate a witness, the witness to the rape." Trivette continued:

> All Janet Siclari wanted to do was to hear and smell the ocean one more time before she went home, back to New Jersey. That is all she wanted to do. Now we tried to show you as much as we could about her. We tried to show you

what kind of a person we believe she was, a daughter and a sister and a wonderful friend who all these folks over here [referring to her family and friends seated behind the state's table] cannot begin to ever understand why this happened. No matter what. We can't make it right for them. There's nothing we can do. We tried to tell you about her.

But the one thing we have never been able to do is tell you is to let you hear her voice, have we? We have never been able to do that throughout this whole process and throughout this whole trial. But I submit to you that we have…provided her with a voice.…We ask you to find Thomas Jabin Berry guilty of both first-degree murder and first-degree rape.

IN HIS CLOSING ARGUMENT, defense attorney John Graham sought to poke holes in the state's argument.

Graham noted that in Bob Siclari's statements to investigators the day of the killing, and, again, almost a year later, on August 6, 1994, he had expressed his suspicions that somebody was waiting right outside their hotel room door in the early morning hours, shortly before Janet was killed, when she stopped by their hotel room.

Graham walked tenderly, knowing that Bob Siclari had established himself to the jury as a sympathetic witness. He "is a good, very decent man" who had been through unfathomable suffering, Graham said, but he indicated Siclari's statements on the witness stand were at odds with his original statements about someone outside their hotel room door.

Graham mentioned the two Miller Lite beer cans found in the Carolinian parking lot by the rental car Janet had driven on the last night of her life, the car she had given Randy Powers a ride home in, implying that Powers might have been the killer. "She had somebody with her, that they sat there and that they drank those beers. And

Berry in court. *Drew C. Wilson.*

if that is true then you have to look to the testimony of Randy Powers," Graham said.

Shortly thereafter, Graham moved to the DNA evidence, the powerful link to his client. He argued that DNA "proves identity" but "DNA doesn't necessarily prove rape or murder." The state, he said, "proved that there was a DNA match and that Janet Siclari was murdered. I don't think they have proven beyond a reasonable doubt, based on these questions, that Jabin Berry murdered her, and I would ask you to think about these questions and find him not guilty. Thank you very much."

> *So if I get to wear the white hat one day and step up from the prosecutor's table and point the finger at a defendant, boy, I would love to have this case because, you know, I could send you back there* [to the jury room] *in* State vs. Randy Powers *and I could get you all to chew on that for a good long time.*
> —Defense attorney Mike Sanders, in his closing argument.

Graham's co-counsel, Mike Sanders, then made his close. He, too, pointed the finger at Randy Powers. Powers was furious that night, Sanders argued, and he had a plan: to ambush his girlfriend, Faith Hopkins. Powers, Sanders noted, "testified that he was going to break into her room. He was going to go through the window, commit a burglary, a felony, and wait inside her room for her." Sanders noted that Powers had a knife, and that at his workplace, two and a half weeks after the murder, a knife was found in a laundry bin that had not been emptied since before the murder.

And while prosecutors had contended Faith and Janet didn't look alike, Sanders maintained there were strong similarities between the two. Both had brown hair that they wore in similar fashion, he said, and both wore white shorts and a blue top the night Janet was slain. Sanders said, "Combine that with this: Randy Powers' alcohol use. You all know goodness well he was drunk that night. He was drinking and he got drinking harder once his girlfriend came into the Port O' Call and started dancing with another man."

"He was drunk and that immediately goes to two things," Sanders argued. "Number one, a case of mistaken identity, which is completely understandable in this situation. Number two, as you all know, is that alcohol use fuels anger. It makes you do things or elevates anger that you would not normally do."

A few drinks can also calm many a soul, instead of elevating their anger, but Sanders was on a roll.

He touched on other points and continued:

> If Randy Powers is so trustworthy, if this guy who wouldn't tell us [the defense] where he is, is so trustworthy, who would not talk to the defense or tell us where he could be located but who amazingly showed up voluntarily for the state, then why hasn't the state, knowing—the state had to know we were going to go after Randy Powers because the evidence makes you go after Randy Powers—why have you not heard from his girlfriend, Faith Hopkins, the one he allegedly had a confrontation in the parking lot with? That was a nice little alibi to the police because that put him in front of the hotel instead of at the back at the time of the murder. The only problem is, you haven't heard from her [Faith].
>
> Why haven't you heard from Shawn Herpin, who was the night clerk....The state listed him on their witness list....Why haven't you heard from him to say that Janet came into the hotel alone? And why haven't you heard from Randy Powers' roommates, the people who would have allegedly verified that he came back in later that night, went on to bed? You can reasonably infer that the reason you have not heard from these people is that they don't back him up.
>
> ADA Trivette: Objection.
>
> Judge Tillett: Ladies and gentlemen, you will be guided by our own recollection of the evidence.

Sanders continued, arguing that Powers had told "four different stories" to investigators:

> Now what do you all think the state of North Carolina would be doing to my client other than stringing him up and hanging him from the yardarm right now if he had told the police four different stories? They would be

arguing to you up one side and down the other about how that is a classic indication that you have committed a crime, when you have inconsistent statements to the police.

What can I do? What can I add to my case against Randy Powers? Randy Powers told four different stories to the police. Four different stories.…Now if that is an innocent man, you all will have to decide. But I submit to you that when you are confronted with a woman you killed, you are not thinking clearly.…

So if I get to wear the white hat one day and step up from the prosecutor's table and point the finger at a defendant, boy, I would love to have this case because you know I could send you back there [to the jury room] in *State vs. Randy Powers* and I could get you all to chew on that for a good long time.

And if what I have just said to you would cause you to chew on anything, then in this case you have a reasonable doubt.

We all feel bad. I'm not going to talk down to this family. I am just like Mr. Graham: It's a solemn occasion that brings us here. But these murder cases are like this. It tests what we are made of and it tests what you are made of. Thank you.

The defense rested. Their client had chosen not to take the stand.

Another shot of Berry in court. *Drew C. Wilson.*

If he wanted to, his lawyers would have no doubt advised against it, as defense lawyers do in most murder trials. The defense lawyers had done their damnedest and raised several valid questions. But had they persuaded the jury that even though their client's semen was a DNA match to that found in Janet, the sex might have been consensual and someone else had killed Janet?

Judge Tillett recessed the court for lunch.

THE JURY BEGAN ITS deliberations at 2:24 p.m. on Tuesday, January 26. A little over three hours later, at 5:44 p.m., the jury sent a question out to the judge: "May jurors examine items, specifically pictures entered into evidence?"

Judge Tillett asked the lawyers for their responses. The prosecution and the defense both indicated no problems with the jury's request, but defense attorney Graham asked, "Judge, is there a specific exhibit that has been enumerated?"

Judge Tillett relayed the request to the jury, which sent out a note detailing its request: the close-up view of the paper bag found near the body, the photo of the body showing what the town maintenance workers who discovered it saw and "the close-up view showing Ms. Siclari clutching the shorts to her throat."

The judge conferred with the attorneys on the photos, then, at 6:02 p.m., allowed the jurors to review them in open court. A few minutes later, the jurors indicated they were satisfied. At 6:12 p.m., Judge Tillett returned the jury to its chambers.

Thirty-five minutes later that Tuesday, after a total of more than four hours of deliberations, the jury returned with its verdict: guilty of first-degree murder and first-degree rape. Berry laid his head down on an arm. His mother put her hands over her face and sobbed.

Janet's family "cried tears of relief and joyfully hugged each other," the *Coastland Times* reported. "We're happy with the jury's decision," Bob Siclari told the newspaper. "We're somewhat relieved. It's been six years, but it's been six long tough years."

Charles Cameron, who'd succeeded Lonnie Dickens as police chief, told the paper: "Literally thousands of hours were invested in this case since the murder. It's the only thing we ever wanted for us, for the Siclari family and for the state, was to have our day in court and to present our evidence."

Judge Tillett recessed court until the following morning at nine thirty, when attorneys would begin the second phase of the trial, arguments for and against the death penalty.

The defense faced a special challenge. The jury clearly hadn't bought their contention that Randy Powers may well have been the killer, and it was sold on the DNA match. Jurors might have seen Berry as remorseless and may have even been angry with him.

14
MOTHER VS. MOTHER AS THE STATE PUSHES FOR THE NEEDLE

I don't wish it on any mother, any mother, to lose a child in this fashion through such a vicious, vicious attack. It's not fair.
—*Janet's mother, Damy Daber, during the sentencing hearing*

Well, I think Jabin sometimes wishes he was a little boy again. When he is around me he loves the attention that I give him and I try to give him extra attention because he was so abused.
—*Jabin Berry's mother, Doris M. Berry, during the sentencing hearing*

The next morning, ADA Robert Trivette began the sentencing phase by calling to the stand Janet's mother, Damy Daber. He asked her about the outpouring of kind words she'd received in the wake of Janet's murder. "Did that mean a lot to you, those people saying those things about your daughter?"

Daber replied:

> Oh, oh people call me from all over, from the beach where she was, people that I didn't even know and they used to say to me, "You must be so proud, Ms. Siclari, to have a daughter like her, you brought up a daughter to be so—she was so respected all over. She was a real lady, a precious girl."

A few minutes later, Trivette asked, "Ms. Daber, when you found out that she was dead, how did you feel?"

Daber answered:

> There's no word to express. My heart, bleeding on the inside. Even though it's six years ago, it's just like it was yesterday. I don't wish it on any mother, any mother, to lose a child in this fashion through such a vicious, vicious attack. It's not fair.

Trivette   Is your life the same now?

Daber   Never, never will, never be the same.

The defense, wisely, chose not to cross-examine Ms. Daber. The state rested its witness testimony for the death penalty with the powerful, gut-wrenching words of Janet's mother.

CONVERSELY, DEFENSE ATTORNEY JOHN Graham presented Jabin Berry's mother, Doris M. Berry, as his witness in making the defense case against the death penalty. Like all good defense attorneys, Graham sought to humanize his client for the jury so they might see him as the troubled child he'd been rather than the monster the prosecution made him out to be. To build such arguments, North Carolina has a robust system of mitigation specialists who work like a supportive family through the state's Indigent Defense Services program. They dive into school records, social service records and many others to establish mitigating factors going back to a defendant's childhood. "Mitigation factors are not excuses, they are reasons for life," a defense lawyer recently said. On Berry's case was one of the best of

Berry in court. *Drew C. Wilson.*

the mitigation specialists, Nancy Pagani, who'd diligently and thoroughly explored Jabin Berry's background.

Graham and Sanders had worked closely with Pagani, and Graham drew from her work as he asked Ms. Berry about her earliest memories of Jabin and Luther, her husband and Jabin's father. Ms. Berry and her husband had divorced when Jabin was about eleven, she testified, and the father had later died. Ms. Berry told the court:

> My husband was not a nice person. He was nice in public, but at home he was very—he drank and he was abusive. Jabin took the brunt of that abuse. I have seen him stand in corners for hours, seen him knocked to the ground by the back of his father's hand. I have seen him beat with belt buckles, not belts, that have left marks on his back. I have stepped in and therefore took a lot of beatings, as many as I could to shield him.

Graham	Was Luther abusive to you as well?
Berry	Yes.
Graham	Was that done in front of the children?
Berry	Well, I tried not to let it be done in front of the children. I always sent the children off in another room and tried to keep them from hearing any screaming and hollering. He [Luther] was mentally, sexually and physically abusive. I don't think any woman anywhere has had as much abuse done to them as I have, including rape.
Graham	Tell us about some of your happier memories of Jabin as a child.
Berry	Jabin was a good child. He hunted a lot in the woods, he was gone a lot. He had a boat that he pushed up and down in the canal. He caught turtles, fish, crab. He tried to avoid being home as much as possible.

Graham showed Berry several idyllic photos from her son's childhood, got her to identify them and had them entered into evidence for the jury to see.

Next, Graham walked Berry through her recollection of her son being sent to jail in nearby Washington, North Carolina, the town called "Little Washington" by locals, when Jabin was about twelve.

Graham	Was that a jail cell designed for adults?
Berry	Yes.
Graham	Tell us about that if you would please.
Berry	It was just a jail cell with a hole in it—where you pass the food to them and they had a commode in there so I guess that is where they did everything.…

Newspaper clipping of a young Jabin Berry with a fish, presented by his trial lawyers trying to save his life. *Dare County Superior Court records.*

In further questioning, Graham established that Jabin Berry had three children by three mothers and had maintained relationships with the children. Berry, his mother said, was "a very devoted father," feeding his

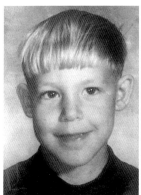
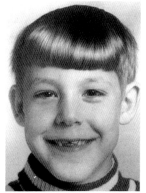

Defense photos of Berry as a child. *Dare County Superior Court records.*

children, bathing them and cooking for them. Her son also wrote poetry, she testified.

One of Jabin Berry's poems was introduced into evidence:

> *Well, here it is midnight and I just can't sleep…*
> *Does anyone miss me or*
> *Do they just say*
> *Well so much for him*
> *He's locked away*
> *I can't explain the pain*
> *That I feel*
> *But It's like fire in my chest*
> *And it sure is real….*

On cross-examination, ADA Trivette drilled down on Doris M. Berry:

Trivette	You said Jabin had a tough childhood. Have you observed some of the effects of that childhood over the years, Ms. Berry?
Berry	Yes I have.
Trivette	Tell us about it.
Berry	Well, I think Jabin sometimes wishes he was a little boy again. When he is around me he loves the attention that I give him and I try to give him extra attention because he was so abused.

Her answer was strong. A lawyer should never ask a question without knowing the answer, as the old saying goes. Trivette, however, quickly regained his footing.

Trivette	Anything else that you have seen?
Berry	Not really.

Trivette	It is safe to say, Ms. Berry, that he's had some problems over the years?
Berry	Oh I believe he's had problems because of this over the years because I have also had problems over this over the years.
Trivette	Isn't it true, Ms. Berry, that you have known that Jabin has had a problem with girls for a long time?
Berry	I have suspected that, yes sir.
Trivette	Isn't it true that the instance where he was locked up in Washington, Little Washington…had to do with a sexual assault of a young child?
Berry	No it was not, I beg your pardon.
Trivette	Isn't it true that it involved a young girl…Ms. Berry?
Berry	May I say what happened there, if I am permitted to do so?
Trivette	You can explain your answer. I'm sure the judge will let you.
Berry	His father used to take him to a little beer joint in Engelhard. That is a little dot on the map. They did not have bathrooms or outdoor toilets at that time, you were virtually in the wilderness. He carried the oldest with him, like I said, I don't know, to ridicule him, get him in front of his buddies, to beat on him. He [Jabin] went around in back of the [place] as did other men, as did women, to use the bathroom. The little girl ran around and said he exposed himself. If that is the fact, I have exposed myself to everyone down there.

Trivette implied through a question that there was a lot more to the incident. Berry denied it. Then he asked: "You have stated before to [SBI] Agent Varnell that you knew that Jabin had problems with young girls, do you recall that?"

Berry   Uh-huh, yes I do, because he [Jabin] thinks sometimes he is still young.

As he continued questioning Ms. Berry, Trivette asked her if she recalled having once said that she thought her son "needed help, that he had a very serious problem."

Berry replied: "I said I think—yes I did say I thought he needed help because in his mind sometimes I think it goes back to the age of 12, where he was traumatized at the age of 12….Does that make any sense to you? I lived through it."

Trivette   Don't you think he [Jabin] needed help, even back then [in the early 1980s]?

Berry   Probably did and so did I, but you don't get it in prison.

With that, Trivette ended his cross-examination.
The defense rested, having called, just as the state, only one witness, a mother.

15
LIFE OR DEATH?

"The Rape of Innocence"

> *There is no more cruel act than the murder of innocence....Except for one, perhaps, and that is the rape of innocence.*
> —*Assistant District Attorney Robert Trivette, in pushing for the execution of Jabin Berry*

By the next morning, as they began arguments for and against the death penalty, the lawyers must have been exhausted, running on adrenaline. Bad lawyers have repeatedly failed in capital cases. But for good lawyers—and those for the both the state and the defense in Janet's case were good—capital trials lasting weeks are like the Olympics. They have to stay fully alert and on their game all day, anticipating their opponent's next move, see around corners, ready to strenuously object as needed, listening intently to their opponent's arguments, all the while scanning their fat case files, trying to read jurors' facial expressions and body language and how best to reach them and mapping their next move, knowing full well that any errors on their part will be scrutinized for years to come by appellate lawyers and judges. And each day when the judge recesses court and the lawyers go home, they can't relax with their families but must go back to those case files and study them late into the night. As they bone up for the sentencing phase, lawyers go over and over their arguments.

Prosecutors study photos of victims in everyday life in their cases, as well as the painful crime scene photos of those victims, preparing to tell their stories, speaking for them, bringing voice to the voiceless. Defense attorneys also study the crime-scene photos, looking for flaws in evidence gathering, even as they introduce photos of their clients as children that will, hopefully, humanize those clients for jurors.

ADA Robert Trivette kicked off the sentencing arguments, contending that Jabin Berry should be executed for killing Janet. He maintained there were two aggravating factors that supported the imposition of the death penalty: "that the murder occurred in the course of another felony, and that felony is the rape" and that Berry had "been convicted of a prior violent felony…taking an indecent liberty with a minor and during the course of committing that offense that he used violence or threatened violence."

Trivette told the jury:

> There is a tie that binds us, I submit, which occurs across generations and all boundaries and which brings us together in our common bond. And that is that the worst possible crimes be punished in the worst possible way. Janet Siclari's death was a terrible way to die. She died in pain. She died struggling to crawl or walk or move back to…the hotel where her family and friends were. Before she died, she breathed in air, the air was trying to go in where there was blood in her lungs, and she, of course, realized, I submit to you, that she was dying and that she was going to die. She was conscious. As Ms. Davis said yesterday, certainly things such as the grief of not having to be able to say goodbye to her mother and her brothers, her father and her friends, crossed her mind. And certainly the unfulfilled dreams of life that we all have.
>
> There is no more cruel act than the murder of innocence, I submit to you. There is no more cruel act in the world. Except for one, perhaps, and that is the rape of innocence. You know rape doesn't have anything to do with sex. Rape is an act of violence. It is an act of power. I submit to you that it's the ultimate objectification of a human being. And I submit to you that when Thomas Jabin Berry looks at another human being, that is what he sees, an object. He doesn't see a human, especially if you are a woman. If you are a woman, to Mr. Berry you are only a potential object to dominate, consume and discard.

Rape is about power and violence, and when it comes to the effect rape has on the soul of a human being it is akin to murder, the effect is to crush the soul. Sometimes the souls are able to recover, sometimes they don't.

On August 28, 1993, Thomas Jabin Berry first tried to murder Janet Siclari's soul by raping her. Then, just like the cuts to her neck that drained her life, he first tried to use his evil to suck out her soul by raping her and then he murdered her.…

We have spent days in this courtroom and every day in this system we call justice and Judge Tillett has gone through great lengths to protect the rights of this defendant, Thomas Jabin Berry. But did he [Berry] care, on August 28, 1993, about the rights of Janet Siclari? No.…

As you weigh your decision, please remember who alone is responsible for all of us being here in this room…as you weigh your decision, surely pity and sympathy will creep into your thoughts. But I suggest to you that pity and sympathy in this matter should be saved for the one who had inflicted on her undeserved pain and suffering on the night she died.

Man is perhaps a perfect—is perhaps the most perfect of all creatures God has created. But when separated from law and justice, he is perhaps the worst. You may have heard the expression that all lives have value. I agree with that, but I submit to you that all lives do not have the same value. I don't think anyone would disagree that Adolf Hitler had anything that came anywhere close to the value of Winston Churchill or Franklin Roosevelt or that the life of Mother Theresa could be matched in any degree by someone such as [the then-leader of Libya, Muammar Gaddafi]. There are differences in the value of life.

Life is a gift and the sentence of death in this case says that life is not cheap and it has value and worth. At this moment you represent the conscience of our community and of our civilization.

To leave you with one last thought: That is that the mark of civilization is the extent to which society upholds the rights of its members, especially the right to life. There is only one appropriate penalty for the willful, unprovoked violation of that right and that is death. By imposing this penalty on those who dare to breach the most basic rule of existence, we affirm the dignity of every other individual. Thank you.

The state rested. Mike Sanders kicked off closing arguments for the defense:

> I have never done this before and hope I never have to do it again. And if I mess up, I ask that you not hold it against him [Jabin]. Jabin and I are about the same age. And as I stand here, I wonder what happened and what went wrong as he was growing up in Engelhard and I was growing up in Elizabeth City and why he is sitting where he is. And I do not suggest to any of you, nor do I want you to take any offense from me or think that I am in any way questioning your judgment in this case on guilt or innocence, because when I took the oath to become a lawyer, part of that oath said that I would respect my fellow lawyers, and I hope I have done that in this case, and the court, and especially the jury and the decisions of the jury. And I do respect that. And you have found him guilty of first-degree murder and of first-degree rape. And the only job I have left to do now is regarding the sentence.
>
> And the weight that you have on your shoulders is much greater than the weight on the shoulders of Mr. Graham and me and I can't imagine....
>
> About all I can do is remind you that he [Jabin] was a little boy. When he caught that fish that day [referring to a photo earlier showed the jury], he wasn't what he is now. Something happened, and I don't know what it was. But the judge is going to instruct you that part of what you can consider by way of mitigation is that there was a poor father-son relationship between Jabin and his father, that he grew up without the benefit of effective parenting skills, that he was a witness to extreme domestic violence, that he did not receive adequate psychological intervention or counseling for his problems, that he was emotionally, sexually and physically abused as a child, and that he is able to express and has a loving relationship with his mother, who you

heard from, and his grandmother. And that he was a father figure. And you can consider those in passing sentence.

I brought with me a book…I always carry. I carry it in my Jeep. I carry it everywhere I go. What it is about is a boy who grew who up in Southport, North Carolina back in the 1920s and '30s. The author of the book, Robert Ruark, and some of you may know, he was in his day one of the world's most famous writers. And what this book is about, for those of you who haven't read it, is his grandfather and the other men in his life, no offense to the ladies, but how someone took the time and made him a man.

Nobody did that for Berry, Sanders suggested.

"And there will come a time when his [Berry's] fate of death will be decided and each of you know that, and I'm asking you that this not be the day," Sanders said. "Thank you."

As deliberations began, Jabin Berry, in a holding cell off the courtroom, reportedly told a bailiff that he would not get the death penalty because a friend of his mother's was on the jury. The juror had not disclosed that connection during jury selection.

Berry reacts during his trial. *Drew C. Wilson.*

After almost two days of deliberations, the jury deadlocked, with the juror in question reportedly being the holdout for life. Then, by law, Tillett, on Friday, January 29, 1999, imposed a life sentence, ordering the bailiffs to have Berry stand.

By a simple twist of fate, Janet Siclari had landed in the wrong place at the wrong time and been murdered. By another simple twist of fate, her killer escaped death.

Tillett, saving Berry's life, decreed:

Berry shows a bit of emotion during his trial. *Drew C. Wilson.*

As to the charge of first-degree rape, the order of this court and judgment [is that] the defendant be imprisoned for a term of life imprisonment in custody of the North Carolina Department of Corrections…as to the charge and crime upon conviction of first-degree murder, it is also ordered that the defendant be imprisoned for a term of life imprisonment in custody of the North Carolina Department of Corrections….This term will run at the expiration of and consecutive to that imposed in the first-degree rape charge….He is in your custody, sheriff.

The defense noted its obligatory appeal. Bailiffs handcuffed Berry and led him out of the courtroom. He would soon be transported by van from his holding cell in Dare County to the mean Central Prison in the state capital of Raleigh, where he would be processed for shipment to a maximum-security prison in the state.

An hour or so later, prosecutors, investigators and Janet's family had a gathering at a Manteo restaurant. They invited defense attorney John Graham. He went, not knowing how he would be received. The reception was gracious, and he appreciated it.

Berry, through attorney Margaret Creasey Ciardella, appealed to the North Carolina Court of Appeals. On May 1, 2001, the court issued its ruling. Regarding the testimony of the Royal Canadian Mounted Police officer, the court wrote, "We hold that although barefoot impression analysis was not yet a reliable science at the time of trial, the admission of such testimony was harmless error."

The court's words were vindication of the defense team's vigorous questioning of the Canadian officer's testimony at trial. It was a small victory. But ultimately, the appeals court effectively ruled that the other evidence outweighed "the harmless error," writing that, "Defendant received a fair trial by a jury of his peers before an able trial judge that was free of prejudicial error. No error."

―――

CNN's show *Forensic Files* did a 2007 segment on the case titled *The Cinderella Story*, the title coming from the lawmen's push to match the shoes found on the crime scene to the killer. Investigators Tom Gilliam and Donnie Varnell come off well in interviews, as does prosecutor Robert Trivette.

Not so much for Jabin Berry. In a prison interview, he is smiling and cocky, maintaining his innocence in Janet's slaying. He claims his sex with Janet was consensual. "I had sex with a lot of people on the beach," he says. "One thing led to another. As a matter of fact I had that happen several times in my life."

When CNN asks Trivette about Berry's contention that his sex with Janet was consensual, Trivette calls Berry a liar and says the evidence is sound.

Janet's mother and Berry's mother died in the years after that broadcast.

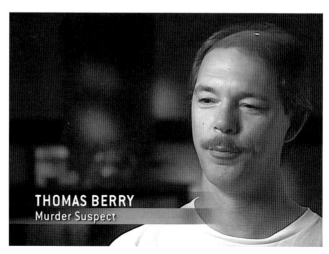

Jabin Berry during his interview with *Forensic Files* on his case. *CNN's* Forensic Files *TV series*.

EPILOGUE

On December 23, 2023, my wife and I drove southwest from our Kitty Hawk base to Engelhard to get a sense of Jabin Berry's hometown. We'd driven through before but wanted to linger this time and get a sense of it through the lens of the research I'd done about the case. It was a fine, sunny afternoon, cool but not cold, with big clouds coasting high up. Engelhard is a wild mix of beauty and hard times, big old fishing trawlers, some beaten by hellacious seas in spots such as the Grand Banks off Newfoundland, docked in canals leading to the Pamlico Sound and gently rocking, boats like the ones Jabin Berry had cruised out on in his working days as a fisherman. Set off against the boats were the lazy small downtown's crumbling buildings, with the exception of a few structures, including a thriving hardware store and the newest and biggest building in town, the local office of the Department of Social Services.

As we walked the tiny downtown, shooting photos, a big man in an old pickup truck slowly glided past, watching us. Finally, he stopped his truck and asked us what we were up to. I told him I was working on a book on Jabin Berry's case. The man exploded, his eyes shooting fire as he moved closer. "I hope you're not on his side."

"Oh hell no," I said. By that point in my investigation, I could honestly say, "Jabin did it, and I'm just nailing it down."

Then the man saw my "No Wetlands/No Seafood" sticker on the kayak in the back of my truck, supporting a longtime nonprofit for commercial fishermen, and loosened up.

Epilogue

The man smiled, extended his hand and gave us a tour of Berry's neighborhood, showing us the canals Berry had played in as a boy, along the way telling us about crimes Berry had committed against his neighbors before he was finally convicted in Janet's case and that Berry should be in prison forever. The man told me that Jabin Berry abused animals and

> *I whipped his ass once when he came at me with a piece of iron. Beat him so bad, whipped his ass, both his eyes were swollen shut and they had to spoon-feed him. The cops interviewed me after the murder, and I told them he abused animals and was a shit. There ain't no law out here.*

As we left Engelhard, I stared up at the blue skies, thinking of Janet and her tragic collision with Jabin Berry and his lawless ways.

As of early 2025, Jabin Berry remained imprisoned, most recently at the Nash Correctional Institution in Nash County, North Carolina, a three-hour drive west from his Hyde County homeland. He did not respond to requests for an interview for this book.

Dare County Court records showed that around 2020, he reached out to the state-supported North Carolina Innocence Inquiry Commission for help with his case.

In appealing to the commission, Berry cited previous problems with SBI lab investigations—and there had been several—but did not cite any strong problems with his case, from my reading of Dare County Superior Court records.

Sources told the author in June 2024 that the commission had found no cause to take up Berry's case because DNA tests of the shoes at the crime scene matched Berry's DNA. A brief letter from the commission to the Dare County Clerk of Court, dated May 20, 2024, supports what the sources told the author. The evidence in the case, the commission wrote, need not be preserved.

Jabin Berry's prison mug shot from 2024. *North Carolina Department of Corrections.*

Epilogue

Robert Trivette (*left*) and John Graham in July 2024 on an Outer Banks beach a few miles north of the Carolinian. Trivette, now the chief district court judge for his area, was one of the two prosecutors against Jabin Berry. Graham was one of Berry's two defense attorneys. Trivette and Graham battled each other in court throughout the trial but remain close friends. *Author photo.*

The commission told the author that their "cases are confidential pursuant to statute" so they would make no comment. The commission's secrecy bars the public's right to know about their deliberations on weak appeals to them and on strong appeals, all of which sometimes go without action from the commission, with no public explanation. The fact that this commission, supported by tax dollars, operates in secrecy is unjust.

Amber Davis Malarney and Robert Trivette, who prosecuted Berry's case, are now both district court judges. John Graham, lead defense counsel on the case, retired in the fall of 2023. His defense partner on the case, Mike Sanders, works on.

My family's oceanfront cottage was a few cottages north of Janet's crime scene, the Carolinian. Many of us locals always try to ride the Beach Road, which hugs the oceanfront, as opposed to the busy bypass

Epilogue

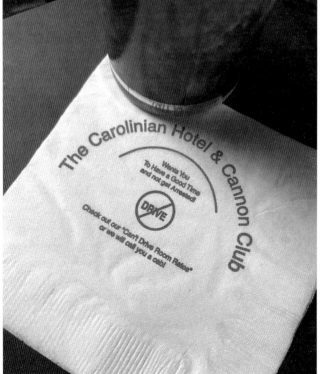

Above: The Carolinian being demolished in the early 2000s. *Drew C. Wilson*.

Left: Napkin from the Carolinian's basement bar a few years before Janet stayed there. *Kathleen Railey*.

Opposite: The Port O' Call today, vacant. *John Railey*.

Epilogue

just to the west, which runs parallel to the Beach Road. We mark points on the Beach Road by long-established mileposts. Our 10 milepost neighborhood was beloved by our family and neighbors—the Robinsons, Gibsons, Grays, Nunemakers, Clemmers and Claytons—growing up in the 1960s and '70s. The Grays' namesake department store was right across the Beach Road from the hotel. We loved to sneak into the Carolinian's pool and play. Cata-cornered across the Beach Road, just north of our cottage, was Nunemaker's grocery, where I worked as a teenager and hung out with the Nunemaker family. We thought it was a safe neighborhood, even as we became adults. Janet's slaying in 1993 shattered our illusions of safety.

On the last night of her life, Janet could have seen my family's cottage from her oceanfront Carolinian room, and we could have seen her window. I have often thought of her going out that night to smoke. I had done the same thing thousands of times in front of our cottage in the years before Janet, staring at the ocean and loving her, just as Janet did. No one had ever threatened me on that beach at night, much less in daylight. We thought we had nothing to fear.

Developers began to tear down the Carolinian in the spring of 2001.

Epilogue

Gone was the beloved landmark that we'd grown up near. My wife, Kathleen, had saved napkins from one of the basement bar's last incarnations just before Janet's time, the Cannon Club. She caught the napkins blowing in the wind, tattered fragments of the old beach we had known, the way we were.

The Port O'Call, Janet's last stop, was still standing in the winter of 2025, vacant for years and for sale.

Across Dare County these days, drugs, particularly cocaine laced with fentanyl, have resulted in overdose deaths and related crime. But I still walk the Nags Head beach alone at night, thinking of Janet and hoping that what happened to her was an aberration, foolishly believing in beach innocence.

Janet helped so many through her medical work, and she would have helped so many others if Jabin Berry had not so brutally cut her life short.

I stare out at the ocean Janet loved, the sea that forever holds all answers.

ACKNOWLEDGMENTS

I interviewed numerous sources for this book, some of whom went on the record, others who preferred to remain anonymous. The fear of Jabin Berry extends past his prison walls. Regarding the on-the-record sources, Tom Gilliam, one of the lead investigators on the case when he was with the Nags Head Police Department, was instrumental in helping me re-create the investigation. Don Rabon, one of the investigators who interviewed Berry, was also crucial. John Graham, Jabin Berry's lead attorney, was instrumental, as was his close friend Robert Trivette, who co-led the prosecution on the case and is now the chief district court judge for his area.

Stephanie Gajar, whose family still owned the Port' O Call in September 2024, was nice enough to give me a quick tour that month of the bar area where Janet spent some of her last hours. I could feel Janet in the rooms with us. Janet's brother Robert Siclari graciously took a cellphone call from me in November 2023. He was, understandably, still pained by his sister's murder and did not talk further. His courageous testimony shows through in the trial transcript.

Former Nags Head Police Officer Jimmy Ray Watts filled in some needed gaps regarding the first hours of the case. Kevin Brinkley, a rookie police officer at the time of the case who later became chief of the department, was also very helpful.

My friend Melissa Gibbs, who grew up in mainland Hyde County several years after Jabin Berry, helped me understand the culture of Berry's formative years. My buddy Ole Anderson, who was part of the original Carolinian family and worked there in the 1960s, was very helpful on the hotel's history. Anita Fletcher, who ran the Comedy Club at the Carolinian at the time Janet was killed, was instrumental in helping me understand the hotel's culture and personalities at that time, as were my friends Buster Nunemaker and Monica Mabry Witt, who worked at the hotel. District Attorney Jeff Cruden, whose jurisdiction includes Nags Head and the rest of Dare County and took office long after this case, was very helpful, as was court reporter Amy Forbis. Claudia Harrington, Pat Cheesman and Kim Montgomery, longtime Dare County Courthouse hands, were also, once again, very helpful.

My buddies Drew Wilson and Walt Gresham, some of the best Outer Banks photojournalists during their time on the Banks, once again generously loaned me their fine photos. My friends Bennett Rose Payne, Claire Fletcher and Liz Granitzki gave me great insight into the Port O' Call restaurant, where Janet and two friends went on the night she was killed. Stuart Parks, formerly of the Outer Banks History Center in Manteo, provided excellent help with photos, as did Katie Daugherty and Tammy Woodward of the center. The center is operated by the State Archives and supported by donations.

Podcaster Rebecca Reisner also provided generous assistance. A CNN documentary on the case, *A Cinderella Story*, was also helpful.

Four lawyers, while not connected to the case, provided wise counsel: Vince Rabil, Chris Mumma, Inga Eglitis Francis and her husband, Rick "Salathiel" Francis. Inga and Rick continue to give me my second home at their cottage back in the woods of Kitty Hawk, and their wonderful rescue boxer, Kelly, is often with me as I write on their deck on moonlit nights. In my native Southampton County, Sandra Marks Councill gave me a great place to edit the manuscript of this book at her wonderful Indian Town home while paddling on my beautiful boyhood river, the Nottoway.

Thanks to longtime Nags Head 10 MP buddies Blades Robinson and his sister Ivy for their beach access from which I would paddle into the ocean on many summer days in 2024, cruising past the site of the old Carolinian, trying to envision Janet's last hours. I would stare up at the heavens, asking Janet for a sign that I was on the right track. I like to think she answered: For two straight days in June 2024, dolphins played right beside my kayak. On other days, I would walk that beach, seeing grandmothers with children or women in their sixties alone, knowing any of them could have been Janet today.

Acknowledgments

I am grateful to my friends Mary Giunca and Angel Khoury for editing this manuscript and to Cam Choiniere for formatting it, along the way throwing in some editing.

Thanks to my friends at Sam & Omies in Nags Head, Carole Sykes and her great team, my ultimate bar for sourcing. And to my buddies at Lagerheads Tavern at Wrightsville Beach, Jim Carter, his top dawg Mark "Rip" Ellington and their team for all their continued support and encouragement.

Thanks to my friends at Arcadia Publishing, Chad Rhoad, Abigail Fleming, Jonny Foster and Kate Jenkins.

My daughter, Molly Fincher, inspired me, as did my sister Mimi Railey Merritt and my late sister Jo Beall, all true beach girls. Ditto on the inspiration for the memory of my late brother, defense attorney Richard E. Railey Jr., who gave me wise counsel on my true crime books. He didn't live long enough to counsel me on this one, but I hope it meets his high bar. My late parents, Dick and Hazel Railey, encouraged me to fight for social and criminal justice.

Most important, as always, my wife, Kathleen, was along for the whole ride, including shooting beautiful photos with me on one potentially dangerous Christmas Eve-eve in Engelhard and providing solid insight from the start, telling me that I had to write this book. Into the mystic, my bride.

BIBLIOGRAPHY

This book is based on Thomas Jabin Berry's trial transcript, his Dare County Superior Court records, Janet's autopsy report, numerous interviews with the lawyers on both sides of his case, detectives, case insiders and articles in the *Coastland Times*. Berry did not respond to requests for an interview. The initial key suspect in the case, who was eliminated by lawmen by the time Berry's DNA testing came through, indicated through a friend that he declined to comment. For that reason, I used the pseudonym Randy Powers to protect his privacy. I did the same for Berry's sexual assault victims before Janet. Their courageous testimony helped put Berry behind bars.

Books by two friends, Amy Pollard Gaw and Beth Ownley Cooper, respectively, *Lost Restaurants of the Outer Banks and Their Recipes* and *Historic Hotels and Motels of the Outer Banks*, supplied great information. The chapter titled "Beechland" in Judge Harry Whedbee's *Legends of the Outer Banks and Tar Heel Tidewater* was very helpful in re-creating Jabin Berry's Hyde County homeland. My friend Jerry Bledsoe's book on a northeastern North Carolina murder, *Blood Games*, was immensely helpful in depicting pathologist Page Hudson.

In setting the scene for this book, I drew from research I'd done for my previous books for The History Press, *The Lost Colony Murder: Seeking Justice for Brenda Joyce Holland*, *Andy Griffith's Manteo: His Real Mayberry* and *Murder in Manteo: Seeking Justice for Stacey Stanton*.

ABOUT THE AUTHOR

Photo by Kathleen Railey.

John Railey has spent much of his life on the Outer Banks. A graduate of the University of North Carolina at Chapel Hill, he is a former editorial page editor of the *Winston-Salem Journal* and investigates mitigating factors in death penalty cases for the state of North Carolina. He has contributed to the *Coastland Times* of the Banks and many other newspapers and has won numerous national, regional and state awards for his writing and reporting. His previous books for The History Press, *The Lost Colony Murder on the Outer Banks: Seeking Justice for Brenda Joyce Holland*, *Andy Griffith's Manteo: His Real Mayberry* and *Murder in Manteo: Seeking Justice for Stacey Stanton*, are top-sellers on the Outer Banks. He is also the author of the memoir *Rage to Redemption in the Sterilization Age: A Confrontation with American Genocide*. He and his friend Nancy Beach Gray, a fellow Outer Banks author, are working on a book about Aycock Brown of Manteo, the almost forgotten photographer who put the Outer Banks on the map in the years after World War II, along the way becoming a romantic Banks legend in his own right.

Visit us at
www.historypress.com